Instructor's Manual and Resource Guide
to Accompany

Psychological Testing and Assessment: An Introduction to Tests and Measurement

Third Edition

Ronald Jay Cohen
Mark E. Swerdlik
Suzanne M. Phillips

Prepared by

Mark E. Swerdlik
Ronald Jay Cohen
Suzanne M. Phillips

Mayfield Publishing Company
Mountain View, California
London • Toronto

International Standard Book Number 1-55934-428-8

Manufactured in the United States of America
10 9 8 7 6 5 4 3 2 1

Mayfield Publishing Company
1280 Villa Street
Mountain View, California 94041

PREFACE

This book is designed as an instructor's companion to the textbook *Psychological Testing and Assessment: An Introduction to Tests and Measurement*, Third Edition, by Ronald Jay Cohen, Mark E. Swerdlik, and Suzanne M. Phillips. In each of the 19 chapters of this book (corresponding to each of the 19 chapters of the text) you will find the following:

A detailed outline of the chapter

Class discussion questions

Class demonstrations

Suggested assignments

A list of media resources

We've successfully used in the college classroom many—though not all—of the teaching tips and other material contained in this resource guide. We would value any feedback you care to give us regarding your own experiences in using either the activities suggested in this guide or any of your own that you have found effective. And we also encourage you to obtain ongoing feedback from your students, feedback that may take the form of a weekly log containing questions or commentary about the material covered. Our objectives in preparing this manual and resource guide parallel our objectives in developing *Psychological Testing and Assessment, Third Edition*, and companion student workbook. Specifically, these objectives are as follows:

1. To provide your students with "do-able" projects and discussion questions pertinent to basic measurement concepts—the better for them to achieve (a) a sense of personal mastery with respect to such concepts; (b) personal experience in relevant data manipulations; and (c) the ability to understand and relate technical terms in professional journals, test manuals, and test reports. Discussion questions can also serve as essay questions for use on exams.

2. To provide a stimulus for mentally grappling with the various legal/ethical—as well as other—issues in measurement.

3. To blend theoretical and applied materials in a way designed to provide the student with a rationale for (and a "hands-on feel" of) the assessment process.

4. To provide case illustrations of the wide range of "real world" contexts in which psychological tests are used.

5. To make students eager to pick up their psychological testing and assessment textbook.

6. To impart a sense of the author's belief in and respect for the psychological testing and assessment enterprise, balanced by a healthy and realistic degree of self-criticism and an eye toward the challenges that still lie ahead.

7. To help make the teaching of this course a bit more enjoyable by giving you more resources at your disposal.

We hope you find the materials available in this resource guide helpful in assisting you in reaching the learning objectives you have articulated for your students. Sincere best wishes for a fulfilling teaching experience!

Mark E. Swerdlik
Ronald Jay Cohen
Suzanne M. Phillips

A test bank is also available in both printed and computer formats. The test bank consists of over 1,200 multiple choice questions that correspond to each chapter of *Psychological Testing and Assessment: An Introduction to Tests and Measurement, Third Edition.* The computer software programs (both Macintosh and IBM-compatible formats) provide the options of editing, adding, deleting, and scrambling the questions to suit the testing requirements of the instructor.

CONTENTS

PART 1
AN OVERVIEW

CHAPTER 1
Psychological Testing and Assessment

Testing and Assessment
    Testing and Assessment Defined
    The Tools of Psychological Assessment
        The test
        The interview
        The portfolio
        The case study
        Behavioral observation
        Other tools
    12 Assumptions in Psychological Testing and Assessment
        Assumption 1: Psychological traits and states exist.
        Assumption 2: Psychological traits and states can be quantified and measured.
        Assumption 3: Various approaches to measuring aspects of the same thing can be useful.
        Assumption 4: Assessment can provide answers to some of life's most momentous questions.
        Assumption 5: Assessment can pinpoint phenomena that require further attention or study.
        Assumption 6: Various sources of input enrich and are part of the assessment process.
        Assumption 7: Various sources of error are part of the assessment process.
        Assumption 8: Tests and other measurement techniques have strengths and weaknesses.
        Assumption 9: Test-related behavior sampling predicts non–test related behavior.
        Assumption 10: Present-day behavior sampling predicts future behavior
        Assumption 11: Testing and assessment can be conducted in a fair and unbiased manner.
        Assumption 12: Testing and assessment benefit society.

Who, What, and Why?
    Who Are the Parties?
        The test developer
        The test user
        The testtaker
        Society at large
    What Type of Settings Is Assessment Conducted In and Why?
        Educational settings
        Counseling settings
        Clinical settings
        Business settings
        Other settings

Evaluating the Quality of Tests
    What Is a "Good" Test or Assessment Procedure?
        Reliability
        Validity
        Other considerations
    Reference Sources for Test Information
        Test catalogues
        Test manuals
        Test reviews

CLOSE-UP
  Computer-Assisted Psychological Assessment

EVERYDAY PSYCHOMETRICS
  Psychometrics Defined

CLASS DISCUSSION QUESTIONS

At the end of this chapter, in a section on reference sources for test information, the student finds the following suggested learning experience:

> To gain some hands-on familiarity with these various sources of test information, try this exercise: Select any one test from those listed in the relevant table in your text and see if you can locate at least two published reviews on it. On the basis of those reviews, would you recommend that the test be used for its intended purpose? Why? Be prepared for your next class period to share your experience and questions regarding the process of such test-related library research.

Students' experiences in completing this task—as well as a discussion of the particular types of tests they selected to research—may provide a nice starting-off point for lecture material that more broadly addresses topics such as

- the role of measurement and, more specifically, psychological measurement in society;

- the use of psychological tests in settings as diverse as classrooms, clinical and counseling offices, and the business world;

- tools used in the assessment process such as tests, portfolios, performance-based assessment, the interview, the case study, and behavioral observation

- different formats of tests such as computerized, paper and pencil, and video;

- the parties to the assessment process including the test developer and publishers, the user of tests and other methods of assessment, and the testtaker; and

- the criteria for what constitutes "a good test" including an introductory look at the concepts of norms, reliability, and validity.

Another convenient starting-off point for lecture material is contained in Table 1–1 regarding differences that have traditionally existed in Scholastic Aptitude Test (SAT) scores as a function of gender and cultural group membership. These data can be examined and the question posed: What issues related to the 12 assumptions in psychological testing and assessment are raised when considering these data? A discussion of these issues can serve as a review of many of the basic concepts presented in this chapter.

Other potential class discussion questions include the following:

1. Have students recall times they have taken group or individual achievement or intelligence tests and
   a. Discuss their general impressions of the test and the testing situation.
   b. Discuss their perceptions of the purposes of administering the tests.
   c. Discuss what outcomes occurred as a result of their participation. What impact (if any) did the testtaking experience(s) have for their lives?
   d. Have students recall how they felt during testing. What factors might have enhanced or negatively affected their performance? What sources of error may have been operating?
   e. What do they consider characteristics of a "good" test? Of a "bad" test?

2. Ask students to discuss in the same contexts as above examples of their experiences with other types of tests such as those used in counseling, business, professional credentialing, program evaluation or psychological theory building, and the legal process.

3. Choose a particular setting (e.g., legal or educational), and ask students to relate some interesting experience they had with respect to some tool of assessment other than a test (such as an interview or behavioral observation). Discuss the possible sources of error variance in the process.

4. As a class, brainstorm as many different measuring units as possible that may have application to psychological measurement; have students explain why. Identify those that appear related to psychological measurement.

5. Compare and contrast the concepts of psychological testing and psychological assessment. Give examples of each from your own life experiences (e.g., group achievement test in school or assessment for selection to a particular college or university). As a psychologist, which approach would you prefer in evaluating clients or applicants? What are the legal implications of each? How do your authors define psychological assessment and psychological testing?

6. Have students give different examples of test formats (e.g., computerized tests). Have them discuss their experiences with computerized tests. How do the advantages of computer-assisted psychological assessment discussed in Chapter 1 from the standpoint of the test user compare to their perceptions as the testtaker?

7. Discuss more recent examples of traits given in the chapter (e.g., androgynous, New Age). Have students identify others. Discuss characteristics that would classify each as a trait.

8. Discuss the 12 assumptions of psychological testing. Give additional examples of each. For example, (Assumption #11) Testing and assessment can be conducted in a fair and unbiased manner: Using Table 1–1, discuss the issue of how well, in the students' view, the SAT (or other college aptitude tests) lives up to this assumption? Discuss the issue of the rights of test users. Do test users have rights? For example, do testtakers have the right to be told the purpose of testing? Should whether or not they be told be dependent on the age of the testtaker? (See Smith [1995] for a draft of the rights of testtakers developed by the Joint Committee on Testing Practices). The rights apply to the use of tests in all settings (i.e., college entrance exams, intelligence tests in schools, employment testing) except classroom testing. Testing and assessment benefits society. Have your students give examples of ways they believe testing and assessment benefit society. Entertain discussion of views that suggest that it does not benefit society.

9. Have the students review the list of possible variables on which testtakers may differ when engaging in the psychological assessment enterprise (e.g., the amount of anxiety, willingness to cooperate, extent to which they have received prior coaching, etc.). Have the students give examples of situations in which they exhibited one or more of these characteristics and how it impacted their performance. Can they think of others to add to the list?

10. How might the concept of psychological assessment be applied to settings such as business/industry, schools, mental health? What would be the purpose of psychological assessment in each setting?

11. If a psychologist were to conduct a case study on one of your students, what sources of information would be appropriate to include?

CLASS DEMONSTRATIONS

1. Bring to class various test/measurement reference books such as *The Eleventh Mental Measurements Yearbook* (Kramer & Conoley, 1992), *The Supplement to the Eleventh Mental Measurements Yearbook* (Conoley & Impara, 1994), and *Test Critiques, Volume X* (Keyser & Sweetland, 1994), and one or more test manuals. Another option would be for your students to take a field trip to the library in order to locate these reference books and others described in the chapter. Either you or the librarian can provide background on the uses of the various sources.

2. Organize a panel of members of your department who represent different specialty areas in psychology. Have them each speak briefly to how their specialty uses psychological tests and assessment.

3. Contact your local police department or a large corporation and determine if any video assessment is used in the training of their personnel. If so, arrange for a guest speaker to come and discuss how this tool of psychological assessment is used.

4. Contact your campus testing and assessment center or office for students with disabilities and inquire if they use any innovative tools for assessment of students with disabilities. If so, perhaps someone could visit your class to demonstrate these tools.

5. Refer your students to a reprinted copy of *Code of Fair Testing Practices in Education* (Joint Committee on Testing Practices, 1988) in Chapter 2. Briefly discuss the 21 points and have students give examples of possible violations based on their personal experiences. This discussion can be expanded after the students have read Chapter 2.

6. Have the class take the self-administered test included in the section of Chapter 1, Everyday Psychometrics. Follow-up discussion can include such questions as What did the test reveal, if anything? Based upon their reading of Chapter 1, what issues would need to be investigated to determine if this test of "Do you have what it takes to be a successful writer?" is a "good" test? Review several of the standards for educational and psychological testing and apply them to this test. Have students review the popular press (e.g., magazines) and bring to class other examples of self-administered tests.

SUGGESTED ASSIGNMENTS

1. Have students contact a local public school district to determine if that district administers minimal competency examinations prior to graduation from junior or senior high school or as a requirement for promotion from grade to grade. If so, what competencies are the test designed to cover? How did the district determine if it was a "good" or "bad" test? What occurs if a student fails the exam? How does the minimal competency exam relate to students enrolled in special education (e.g., classes for the learning disabled, mentally retarded, etc.)?

2. Divide the class into three groups of students (G1, G2, and G3). G1's assignment is to contact the university/college admissions office and inquire about criteria considered in making enrollment decisions. G2 contacts various department chairs to make inquiry regarding the factors considered in making decisions about admission to various graduate programs. G3 interviews nonpsychology students about both of these questions. What common factors emerge and how are they assigned differential weight by the interviewees? Why is it important to consider many factors when making decisions about applicants? What tools of psychological assessment are used in the process? Would they consider the admissions process an assessment? How is the reliability and validity of the process addressed?

3. The text references an estimate that upward of 20,000 psychological, behavioral, and cognitive measures are developed each year. Students are asked to think of one or more psychological tests that they would consider developing. Students should also respond to questions such as What would it measure? For what purposes would it be used? In what settings would it be utilized? For what ages would it be appropriate?

4. Have students contact local business firms to inquire about what kind of tools of psychological measurement, if any, are used for employee selection, retention, promotion, and so on.

5. Have students discuss a job or an occupation that they believe would be particularly amenable to testing (using written or other tools of assessment) for employee selection.

6. Have students try to list all the possible "significant" nonverbal behaviors an interviewer might observe while conducting an interview. Students should specify what type of behavior might be more or less significant in what type of interview. A role-play could be set up with the instructor or another student playing the employer (interviewer) and a student the applicant (interviewee).

7. Have students locate the following reference books in the library and summarize a sample entry for each: *The Eleventh Mental Measurements Yearbook*, *The Supplement to the Eleventh Mental Measurements Yearbook*, *Test Critiques*, and one other reference source listed in the chapter. Summarize a sample entry for each.

MEDIA RESOURCES

ABC's of School Testing (1994, NCME, 30 minutes, color video). Explains basics of testing in the school setting. Developed for parents but provides good introduction to basic issues in testing and assessment. Includes a leader's guide.

Developing Psychometry Skills (AAVP, 53 minutes, VHS Video, b&w). Discusses the topics of measurement of intelligence, aptitude, and emotion. Demonstrates necessary steps involved in developing psychometry skills.

Observation (1993, MS, 27 minutes, VHS Video, color). Provides rationale for observing children and summary of types of naturalistic and subjective observational techniques including the basic components of naturalistic observations. Difficulties encountered in observing and recording are also addressed.

One in a Hundred (1966, ETS, 25 minutes, b&w). Describes how the Educational Testing Service (ETS) constructs a test. Depicts construction of one item in the hundred to be included in the College Board Achievement test in American history and social studies. Although film is dated, steps depicted in the film remain current.

Performance Assessment (1993, AIT, no time listed, VHS Video, color). Provides a summary of the limitations of standardized tests relating to their inability to provide an adequate assessment of valuable educational goals such as cooperation, problem solving, and creativity. Argues for alternative assessment strategies that are performance based.

Standardized Tests: An Educational Tool (1961, PSt, 25 minutes, color). Concepts of reliability, validity, norms, distributions, and test interpretation are discussed in the context of an eighth-grade teacher selecting an appropriate group test to measure the reading abilities of her students. Although film is dated, discussion of concepts is relevant today.

The Test (1980, INU, 11 minutes, color). Explores positive ways of looking at standardized tests and illustrates ways to prepare for the tests, such as by familiarizing yourself with the manual, and how to give students practice sessions.

REFERENCES

American Psychological Association. (1985). *Standards for educational and psychological testing*. Washington, DC: Author.

Eyde, L. D., Robertson, G. J., Krug, S. E., Moreland, K. L., Robertson, A. G., Shewan, C. M., Harrison, P. L., Porch, B. E., Hammer, A. L., & Primoff, E. S. (1993). *Responsible test use: Case studies for assessing human behavior*. Washington, DC: American Psychological Association.

Keyser, D. J., & Sweetland, R. C. (Eds.). (1994). *Test critiques* (Vol. X). Austin, TX: Pro-ed.

Conoley, J., & Kramer, J. (Eds.). (1992). *The eleventh mental measurements yearbook*. Lincoln, NE: Buros Institute of Mental Measurements.

Conoley, J., & Impara, J. (Eds.). (1994). *The supplement to the eleventh mental measurements yearbook.* Lincoln, NE: Buros Institute of Mental Measurements.

Joint Committee on Testing Practices. (1988). *Code of fair testing practices in education.* Washington, DC: Author.

Smith, D. (March, 1995). What rights do test takers have? Paper presented at the meeting of the National Association of School Psychologists, Chicago, IL. (Available from Dr. Douglas Smith, Department of Psychology, University of Wisconsin-River Falls, River Falls, WI 54022-2881.)

CHAPTER 2

Historical, Cultural, and Legal/Ethical Considerations

An Historical Perspective
    Antiquity to the Nineteenth Century
    The Nineteenth Century
    The Twentieth Century
        The measurement of intelligence
        The measurement of personality
        Measurement in various settings

Culture and Assessment
    Verbal Communication
    Nonverbal Communication
    Standards of Evaluation

Legal/Ethical Considerations
    The Concerns of the Public
    The Concerns of the Profession
        Test-user qualifications
        Testing people with disabilities
        Computerized test administration, scoring, and interpretation
    The Rights of Testtakers
        The right of informed consent to testing
        The right to be informed of test findings
        The right to have the least stigmatizing label
        The right to have findings held confidential
    Psychological Tests in the Courtroom

CLOSE-UP
    Tests, Assessment, and Culture

EVERYDAY PSYCHOMETRICS
    Test Use, Base Rates, and Jury Impressions

CLASS DISCUSSION QUESTIONS

In the concluding section of this chapter, the subject of test-user qualifications is broached with questions such as the following:

    Who should be privy to psychological test data?

    Who should be able to purchase psychological test materials?

    Who is qualified to administer, score, and interpret psychological tests?

    What level of expertise in psychometrics is required in order to be qualified to administer each type of test?

Classroom discussion of such questions may prove to be a thought-provoking springboard to related legal/ethical issues discussed in the chapter including:

- the concerns of the public including (too) often heard comments such as "the only things tests measure is the ability to take tests";

- the concerns of the profession including guidelines from the professional organizations regarding the development and use of tests; and

- the various ways that tests may potentially be misused.

With respect to the latter point, one might discuss abuse of English language tests with non–English-speaking people (a commonplace occurrence in turn-of-the century America at the Ellis Island immigration processing center) or the current abuse of assessment procedures in some foreign countries where dissidents (as well as others the government wants to silence) may be "diagnosed" and forcibly hospitalized on "psychiatric" grounds.

Some other discussion questions are as follows:

1. What is the modern-day significance of the competitive testing for civil service jobs that existed in ancient China?

2. What were Hippocrates's views about personality assessment and treatment, and how did they differ from the prevailing beliefs of that period in history? How were his views similar or dissimilar to current thinking in the area of psychodiagnosis and assessment?

3. Galton is viewed as one of the most influential figures in the history of the field of psychological measurement. Why?

4. Discuss the relationship between a particular culture's views of the etiology and treatment of abnormal behavior and its psychological assessment procedures.

5. Discuss the impact of culture, including verbal and nonverbal communication and standards for evaluation, on the psychological assessment process. Ask the students to share experiences they might have had personally or examples others have experienced during which cultural factors might have impacted the results.

6. If you were applying for a job as a research assistant with the Department of Psychology, would you want to have the employment decision based solely on the interview? Behavioral observation? Written test? Which? All? Why?

7. What are the advantages and disadvantages of the truth-in-testing legislation to you as a testtaker? As a test user?

8. Does anyone in the class believe that he or she has had firsthand experience with unethical and improper testing procedures? Why? What action might have prevented this?

9. When you read about the history of the etiology, assessment, and treatment of psychological disorders, some of it may seem a bit outrageous. What aspects of our current psychometric practices might students of the future perceive to be a bit outrageous? What aspects of current psychiatric practice will stand the test of time?

10. "Necessity is the mother of invention." How does this statement relate to the development of intelligence and personality tests in Europe and in America in the early part of the century?

11. "There ought to be a law . . . " Let's play "The Sentence Completion Game" and discuss what legislation students would like to see passed with respect to psychological testing.

12. Discuss the use of psychological tests at Ellis Island. For what purpose were they administered? Was this an example of psychological testing or psychological assessment? What legal and ethical implications/questions did this testing raise?

13. Why is it important to have published standards for educational and psychological tests? What are some of the abuses that the standards are intended to prevent? The instructor can bring to class a copy of the *Standards for Educational and Psychological Testing* (1985), or the revision that is currently "in press" and to be published by the American Psychological Association, and an example of published standards of ethical behavior that specifically addresses aspects of responsible test development and use (e.g., National Association of School Psychologists [1994], American Association for Counseling and Development [1988]). Give example principles from these documents and have students relate their own experiences with tests and the assessment process that would be either consistent or inconsistent with the particular example. A valuable resource for use in this discussion of standards for educational and psychological testing is *Responsible Test Use: Case Studies*

for Assessing Human Behavior (Eyde, Robertson, Krug, Moreland, Robertson, Shewan, Harrison, Proch, Hammer, & Primoff, 1993) published by the American Psychological Association. This book contains 78 case studies illustrating the various principles of responsible test use drawn from the various standards published by the professional organizations.

14. Refer your students to a reprinted copy of *Code of Fair Testing Practices in Education* (Joint Committee on Testing Practices, 1988) in Chapter 2. Discuss the 21 points and have students give examples of possible violations based on their personal experiences.

15. Refer the students to the Everyday Psychometrics section in this chapter. Discuss what the students believe might "stick in the minds of the jury" about the psychologist's testimony. Based on legal and ethical principles, what would have been the irresponsibilities of the test user (the psychologist) in this case? What populations were being compared in this example?

CLASS DEMONSTRATIONS

1. Invite a knowledgeable special education due process hearing officer and/or attorney to class to discuss the implications of state and federal law for psychological testing practices.

2. Invite a personnel director/industrial psychologist to class to discuss the implications of recent court decisions on employment selection procedures.

3. Invite your college or university coordinator of disability concerns or director of the office of students with disabilities to class to discuss the passage of Americans with Disabilities Act of 1990 and its implications for students at your college or university.

4. Bring to class a computerized test administration, scoring, and/or test interpretation printout (or your personal computer, if possible), and have the students actually take the test, score the test, and/or interpret the test themselves using the computer. Discuss the legal and ethical implications of the use of such computerized aids.

5. Invite to class a school psychologist or another person (e.g., coordinator of multicultural or bilingual education) involved in determining the primary language of students prior to conducting a psychological assessment. Ask this person to discuss the issues related to culture including language and nonverbal communication that may affect the results of a psychological assessment. How is the primary language of the student determined prior to initiating the assessment? Are translators used and what are the advantages and disadvantages of using them?

6. Relating to the chapter Close-Up, bring to class examples of "culture-specific tests" such as the Black Intelligence Test of Cultural Homogeneity (Williams, 1975) or Cultural/Regional Uppercrust Savvy Test (Herlihy, 1977). What are the problems with these tests? Also refer back to the Close-Up and discuss the students' responses to the questions raised concerning the examples of culture-specific items included in previously used intelligence tests.

SUGGESTED ASSIGNMENTS

1. Divide the class in half. One half will read Walter Lippmann's articles "The Abuse of Tests" (November, 1922) and "The Mental Age of Americans" (October, 1922) in the *New Republic*. The other half will read Lewis Terman's article in the *New Republic*. Based on the arguments contained in each, the class holds a debate. Did the outcome of the debate reflect the opinion of the readership of the *New Republic* in 1922 as reported in the text? Ask each group to review the November, 1965 (Vol. 20) special issue of the *American Psychologist* and include in the debate the various concerns expressed at the Congressional hearings.

2. Have students interview the personnel director/industrial psychologist for a local corporation. Determine what effect the *Griggs v. Duke Power Company* (1971), *Albemarle Paper Company v. Moody* (1976), and *Allen v. District of Columbia* (1993) court decisions have on employee testing/selection procedures.

3. Relating to the chapter Close-Up, Psychological Testing at Ellis Island, have students, over a weekend, question their parents and grandparents to determine if they can share any recollections of stories they might have heard of their ancestors/relatives (e.g., great-grandparents) immigrating to this country and entering at Ellis Island. Do any of the stories relate to tests they might have taken upon entering the United States?

MEDIA RESOURCES

The Americans with Disabilities Act (ADA): New Access to the Workplace (1991, UMN, 39 minutes, color, VHS). Explains the ADA, which bans discrimination against people with disabilities by employers. Dramatizes the handling of hiring and employment issues that may be encountered.

The Larry P. Case (1978, INHURTS; INUAV, 30 minutes, color). Reviews the background, content, and progress of the Larry P. case. Because the production date is 1978, the instructor should supplement with updated material included in the text as well as other sources. (See Sattler, 1988.)

Testing—None of the Above (1978, UWISC, 33 minutes, color). Through the use of a dream sequence dramatizes the basic misconceptions and the negative impact of norm-referenced standardized testing.

Check with your state education agency and local citizens with disabilities advocacy groups for videotapes, slide/tape presentations, and other media dealing with the issue of legal requirements for psychological evaluations.

REFERENCES

Eyde, L. D., Robertson, G. J., Krug, S. E., Moreland, K. L., Robertson, A. G., Shewan, C. M., Harrison, P. L., Porch, B. E., Hammer, A. L., & Primoff, E. S. (1993). *Responsible test use: Case studies for assessing human behavior*. Washington, DC: American Psychological Association.

Herlihy, B. (1977). Watch out, IQ myth: Here comes another debunker. *Phi Delta Kappan, 59*, 298.

Joint Committee on Testing Practices. (1988). *Code of fair testing practices in education*, Washington, DC: Author.

Sattler, J. M. (1988). *Assessment of children*. (3d ed.). San Diego, CA: Jerome Sattler Publisher.

Williams, R. (1975). The BITCH-10: A culture-specific test. *Journal of Afro-American Issues, 3*, 103–116.

PART 2
THE SCIENCE OF PSYCHOLOGICAL MEASUREMENT

CHAPTER 3
A Statistics Refresher

Scales of Measurement
    Nominal Scales
    Ordinal Scales
    Interval Scales
    Ratio Scales
    Measurement Scales in Psychology

Describing Data
    Frequency Distributions
    Measures of Central Tendency
        The arithmetic mean
        The median
        The mode
    Measures of Variability
        The range
        The interquartile and semi-interquartile range
        The average deviation
        The standard deviation and variance
    Skewness
    Kurtosis

The Normal Curve
    Area Under the Normal Curve

Standard Scores
    z Scores
    T Scores
    Other Standard Scores
        Normalized standard scores

CLOSE-UP
    Error of Measurement and the True Score Model

EVERYDAY PSYCHOMETRICS
    The Normal Curve and Psychological Tests

CLASS DISCUSSION QUESTIONS

A provocative question to open discussion related to this chapter relates to the challenge given the student in the text section labeled "Describing Data":

> Suppose you have magically changed places with the professor teaching this course and you have just administered an examination that consists of 100 multiple-choice items (where one point is awarded for each correct answer). The scores for the 25 students enrolled in your class could theoretically range from 0 (none correct) to 100 (all correct). Assume it is the day after your examination and you are sitting in your office with the data listed in Table 3–1. One task at hand is to communicate the test results to your class in a way that will best assist each individual student in understanding how he or she performed on the test in comparison to all of the other testtakers in the class. How do you accomplish this objective?

At the end of the chapter, students are again encouraged to give some thought to this task and come to class prepared with some answers:

> It may be helpful at this time to review this statistics refresher to make certain that you indeed feel "refreshed." Apply what you have learned about frequency distributions, graphing frequency distributions, measures of central tendency, measures of variability, the normal curve, and standard scores to the question posed in the chapter. How would you communicate the data from Table 3–1 to the class? Which type of frequency distribution might you use? Which type of graph? Which measure of central tendency? Which measure of variability? Might reference to a normal curve or to standard scores be helpful? Why or why not?

> Come to the next class session prepared with your thoughts on the answers to these questions—as well as your own questions regarding any of the material that could still stand a bit more explanation. We will be building on your knowledge of basic statistical principles in the chapters to come, and it is important that such building be on a rock-solid foundation.

Your students are asked to get involved in the subject matter by doing more than merely reading. As a way to reinforce the concepts presented, have them calculate the various statistics presented in this chapter using the examination data presented in the table. Computations and various methods for class presentation are listed below. Computational formulas can be found in the chapter and/or the companion *101 Exercises in Psychological Testing and Assessment, Third Edition.*

Mean: Arithmetic average of the scores.
First formula for computing arithmetic mean of student's examination data in the table.

Score
(number correct)

78
67
69
63
85
72
92
67
94
62
61
44
66

87
76
83
42
82
84
51
69
61
96
73
79

$$\text{SUM} = \frac{1803}{25} = 72.12$$

Mean = 72.12

Second method for computing arithmetic mean from frequency distribution:

Frequency Distribution of Scores from Your Test

Score	f (frequency) f(x)	X
96	1	96
94	1	94
92	1	92
87	1	87
85	1	85
84	1	84
83	1	83
82	1	82
79	1	79
78	1	78
76	1	76
73	1	73
72	1	72
69	2	138
67	2	134
66	1	66
63	1	63
62	1	62
61	2	122
51	1	51
44	1	44
42	1	42

$$\Sigma x = \frac{1803}{25} = 72.12$$

Median: Middle score of the distribution.

Frequency Distribution
of Scores from your Test

Score	*f* (frequency)
96	1
94	1
92	1
87	1
85	1
84	1
83	1
82	1
79	1
78	1
76	1
73	1
72	1 (the middle score)
69	2
67	2
66	1
63	1
62	1
61	2
51	1
44	1
42	1

Median = 72

Arrange scores in a frequency distribution. Count up 12 and count down 12 using the frequencies; middle score is 72.

Mode is the most frequently occurring score in the distribution.

Frequency Distribution
of Scores from your Test

Score	*f* (frequency)
96	1
96	1
94	1
92	1
87	1
85	1
84	1
83	1
82	1
79	1
78	1
76	1
73	1
72	1

69	2
67	2
66	1
63	1
62	1
61	2
51	1
44	1
42	1

Mode = 69, 67, and 61; this distribution is tri-modal.

Range: The range of a distribution is equal to the difference between the highest and the lowest scores.

Frequency Distribution
of Scores from your Test

Score	f (frequency)
96	1
94	1
92	1
87	1
85	1
84	1
83	1 Q3
82	1
79	1
78	1
76	1
73	1
72	1 Q2
69	2
67	2
66	1
63	1 Q1
62	1
61	2
51	1
44	1
42	1

Range = 54

Highest score (96) − lowest score (42) = 54

Interquartile range: See *101 Exercises in Psychological Testing and Assessment, Third Edition,* for a convenient method of calculating.

Average Deviation (AD): The average deviation of all the scores in the distribution from the mean.

Frequency Distribution of Scores from Your Test

Score	f (frequency)	$x - \bar{x}$
96	1	23.88
94	1	21.88
92	1	19.88
87	1	14.88
85	1	12.88
84	1	11.88
83	1	10.88
82	1	9.88
79	1	6.88
78	1	5.88
76	1	3.88
73	1	.88
72	1	.12
69	1	3.12
69	1	3.12
67	1	5.12
67	1	5.12
66	1	6.12
63	1	9.12
62	1	10.12
61	1	11.12
61	1	11.12
51	1	21.12
44	1	28.12
42	1	30.12

Sum of deviation scores = 287.12 divided by 25 = 11.48
Average Deviation (AD) = 11.48

Standard deviation: Is equal to the square root of the average squared deviations about the mean.

Score	f	$x - \bar{x}$	$(x - \bar{x})^2$
96	1	23.88	570.25
94	1	21.88	478.73
92	1	19.88	395.21
87	1	14.88	221.41
85	1	12.88	165.89
84	1	11.88	141.13
83	1	10.88	118.37
82	1	9.88	97.61
79	1	6.88	47.33
78	1	5.88	34.57
76	1	3.88	15.05
73	1	.88	.77
72	1	−.12	.01
69	1	−3.12	9.73
69	1	−3.12	9.73
67	1	−5.12	26.21
67	1	−5.12	26.21
66	1	−6.12	37.45
63	1	−9.12	83.17
62	1	−10.12	102.41
61	1	−11.12	123.65
61	1	−11.12	123.65
51	1	−21.12	446.05
44	1	−28.12	790.73
42	1	−30.12	907.21

$$\frac{4,972.53}{25 \text{ (total scores)}} = 198.90$$

Variance = 198.90

Standard deviation (square root of variance) = 14.10

The article "Methods of Expressing Test Scores" (Test Service Notebook #148 published by the Psychological Corporation) is reprinted in the companion *101 Exercises in Psychological Testing and Assessment, Third Edition*. The chart presented on page 2 of the article can be particularly helpful to students in perceiving the relationships between the various test score statistics presented in this chapter and Chapter 4.

Returning now to the questions posed for class discussion, some acceptable answers are as follows:

Q: "How would you communicate the data from Table 3–1 to the class?"
A: The instructor could initially present a frequency distribution, graph the results, and provide meaningful statistics to help the students interpret their individual scores.

Q: "What type of frequency distribution might you use?"
A: A grouped frequency distribution (see Table 3–3) would facilitate interpretation by your students. This form of presentation will give your students a clearer picture of where they stand in comparison to their classmates. It will also provide you, as the instructor, with a better idea of trends in the data.

However, if you (the instructor of the hypothetical class) intend to compute other statistics (e.g., z scores, means, standard deviation, percentile ranks), a frequency distribution is preferable as it facilitates computation of these statistics. The method of computation/presentation of these statistics, as presented above, utilizes a frequency distribution.

Q: "Which type of graph?"
A: A histogram would provide the most meaningful graphic representation of the data. It represents the simplest graphic representation to understand.

Q: "Which measure of central tendency?"
A: Due to the lack of skewness, the mean would represent the most reasonable measure of central tendency.

Q: "Which measure of variability?"
A: The standard deviation represents the most commonly used index of variability if the mean is the measure of central tendency chosen. If the median is used, the interquartile range is the most common.

Q: "Might reference to a normal curve or standard scores be helpful? Why or why not?"
A: Either reference to a normal curve or a standard score may be helpful depending on the purpose of the presentation and the characteristics of the sample of scores. Standard scores (e.g., z scores, T scores, stanines) are easy to interpret and provide an index of the testtaker's performance relative to others. Computation of several standard scores follows:

z scores (Note: The standard deviation of this set of scores is 14.10.)

X	f	$x - \bar{x}$	$\dfrac{(x - \bar{x})}{14.10} = z$
96	1	23.88	1.69
94	1	21.88	1.55
92	1	19.88	1.40
87	1	14.88	1.05
85	1	12.88	.91
84	1	11.88	.84
83	1	10.88	.77
82	1	9.88	.70
79	1	6.88	.49
78	1	5.88	.42
76	1	3.88	.28
73	1	.88	.06
72	1	−.12	−.008
69	1	−3.12	−.22
69	1	−3.12	−.22
67	1	−5.12	−.36
67	1	−5.12	−.36
66	1	−6.12	−.43
63	1	−9.12	−.65
62	1	−10.12	−.72
61	1	−11.12	−.79
61	1	−11.12	−.79
51	1	−21.12	−1.50
44	1	−28.12	−1.99
42	1	−30.12	−2.14

T scores $= 10z + 50$

Score	f (frequency)	T
96	1	67 (66.90)
94	1	66 (65.50)
92	1	64
87	1	61 (60.5)
85	1	59 (59.1)
84	1	58 (58.4)
83	1	58 (57.7)
82	1	57
79	1	55 (54.9)
78	1	54 (54.2)
76	1	53 (52.8)
73	1	51 (50.6)
72	1	50 (49.9)
69	2	48 (47.8)
67	2	46 (46.4)
66	1	46 (45.7)
63	1	44 (43.5)
62	1	43 (42.8)
61	2	42 (42.1)
51	1	35
44	1	30 (30.1)
42	1	29 (28.6)

It may be helpful to refer to the normal curve if you want to grade on the curve. For example, you may decide that you want to give the top 15 percent an A (above the 85th percentile and more than one standard deviation above the mean), a B to between the 60th and 84th percentile, a C to those between the 20th and 59th, a D to those who earn scores that rank between the 6th and 19th percentile, and an F to those below the 5th percentile. If it is assumed that the scores on the test are normally distributed, there is a precise mathematical relationship between z, T, and other standard scores. If normally distributed, linear z and T scores can be interpreted as they relate to percentiles. You can convert raw scores (number correct) to z scores and then use a chart to convert to percentiles to determine at what point—such as a percentile score—the examinee scored in relationship to the normal curve. You can then use that percentile to assign grades according to the scale designated above. Although normative samples for most standardized tests are very large and their distributions of scores approach normality, most classroom tests for groups of 25 students are not normally distributed and it would not be appropriate to complete the transformations above for typical classroom tests.

Some additional discussion questions follow:

1. Some psychologists do not consider nominal scales a form of measurement. Any ideas why?

2. Most psychological measurement is ordinal in nature. Why?

3. Discuss the types of distributions of data you would expect for the following:
   a. IQ test scores from all pupils enrolled in Illinois schools
   b. IQ test scores from all pupils enrolled in Bayonne, New Jersey, schools
   c. test scores from a very difficult test
   d. a series of 1,000 rolls of the die
   e. college professors' salaries in a university department in which all of the professors have tenure and have been teaching for more than 20 years
   f. test scores from a very easy test

4. You are the union negotiator for a company that has a number of highly paid workers who have been with the company for a very long time. You are trying to negotiate for a substantial raise for next year. Which statistic would you want to use to summarize the average salary of your workers, the mean or the median? Why?

5. List examples of nominal, ordinal, interval, and ratio from your everyday experience. Now list them for each of the following: rankings from a gymnastic meet, height, weight, blood type, major league baseball standings, page numbers for this book, your test grades in this course, your college grade-point average (GPA), IQ scores, and personality test scores.

6. As a follow-up to the discussion in this chapter's Everyday Psychometrics section, discuss examples of psychological traits that the class would not expect to be normally distributed, such as intelligence test scores for university students. Why in each case of a normal distribution presented in this section do the researchers make a special point of stating that the scale under investigation yielded something close to a normal distribution? What are the advantages of knowing that a distribution of a particular trait is normally distributed?

CLASS DEMONSTRATIONS

1. Administer the Attitudes Towards Statistics Scale (Wise, 1985). Using the test-score data, calculate the mean, median, mode, range, interquartile range, and semi-interquartile range, variance, and standard deviation. Which measure of central tendency best represents the distribution of exam scores?

2. Distribute a questionnaire the first session that asks students to list their gender, number of brothers and sisters, height and weight, number of children they would like to have; to pick a number from one to ten, and then to enter a zero if it was an even number and a one if it was an odd number; and to indicate their birth order. This data set can then be used throughout the discussion of statistics to illustrate concepts and provide students with data to use for practice exercises (Jacobs, 1980).

3. Administer a student-designed Student Information Questionnaire (Thompson, 1994) and use data to illustrate statistical concepts presented in the chapter.

4. Have a "Las Vegas Night" in the classroom. One student rolls a pair of dice 75 times while the class records the result of each throw. Make a frequency distribution, grouped frequency distribution, histogram, and frequency polygon of the results. Characterize the distribution using Figure 3–4 as a model. No wagering allowed.

5. The companion student workbook, *101 Exercises in Psychological Testing and Assessment, Third Edition*, also contains a number of exercises to illustrate concepts presented in this chapter.

6. Buck (1991) describes a class demonstration used to illustrate the concepts of measurement error and reliability. Allen (1992) critically evaluates the demonstration pointing out several errors and Buck (1992) responds to these criticisms.

SUGGESTED ASSIGNMENTS

1. A real-life example useful in teaching descriptive statistics is provided by Shatz (1985). Assign it and then discuss it.

2. Have each student review the evening newspaper and/or weekly news magazines looking for news articles or advertisements that include references to the statistics discussed in this chapter. Students will bring in the articles and discuss them during the next class session, focusing on the type of statistics utilized and whether the appropriate one was chosen.

MEDIA RESOURCES

Describing Distributions: Normal Distributions Program #4 (1988, UMN, 30 minutes, color, VHS). Presents ways of describing the shape of a distribution, focusing on the normal curve.

Statistics at a Glance (1972, U of I, 28 minutes, color). An entertaining explanation of frequency distributions, measures of central tendency, and the concepts of variability and correlation.

Mean, Median, Mode (1966, MH, 14 minutes, color). Uses common situations to illustrate the mean, median, and mode.

REFERENCES

Allen, M. J. (1992). Comments on "A demonstration of measurement error and reliability." *Teaching of Psychology, 19,* 111.

Buck, J. L. (1991). A demonstration of measurement error and reliability. *Teaching of Psychology, 18,* 46–47.

Buck, J. L. (1992). When true scores equal zero: A reply to Allen. *Teaching of Psychology, 19,* 111–112.

Jacobs, K. W. (1980). Instructional techniques in the introductory statistics course: The first class meeting. *Teaching of Psychology, 7,* 241–242.

Shatz, M. A. (1985). The Greyhound strike: Using a labor dispute to teach descriptive statistics. *Teaching of Psychology, 12,* 85–86.

Thompson, W. B. (1994). Making data analysis realistic: Incorporating research into statistics courses. *Teaching of Psychology, 21,* 41–43. Copies of Student Information Questionnaire are available from W. Burt Thompson, Department of Psychology, P.O. Box 2208, Niagara University, Niagara, NY 14109-2208.

Wise, S. L. (1985). The development and validation of a scale measuring attitudes toward statistics. *Educational and Psychological Measurement, 45,* 401–405.

CHAPTER 4

Norms, Correlation, and Regression

Norms

CLASS DISCUSSION QUESTIONS

The introduction to this chapter makes reference to the popular notion that "the crazies come out of the woodwork when the moon is full." Mention is then made of the fact that while many correlational studies seem to support this popular belief, few of these studies has been found to be methodologically sound. In this context, the Rotton and Kelly (1985) study might provide a useful starting point for a discussion of the concept of correlation and the critical need for carefully designed measures.

Other potential class discussion questions are as follows:

1. Discuss the various characteristics of norms. What makes for an appropriate norm group? Assume you were developing an entrance test for an auto mechanics school. What type of norm group would be most appropriate for this test?

2. Considering a normal distribution of scores, which of the following are farthest from the mean:

   z score of 1

   Percentile rank of 50

3. For the following decisions, choose which type of measurement, norm-referenced or criterion-referenced, you believe most appropriate:
   a. admission to your university honors program
   b. state licensing/registration as a medical doctor, barber, psychologist
   c. minimal competency exam for graduation from high school
   d. program planning for remedial instruction in reading
   e. grade in your psychological measurement course

4. Drawing upon the discussion of correlation in Chapter 4, choose the most appropriate type of correlation coefficient (Pearson r, Spearman rho, etc.) and diagram what the scatter plots might look like for the following examples:
   a. the relationship between chronological age and intelligence
   b. height and weight
   c. rank order of ACT score and weight

5. Discuss students' experiences using introductory psychology students as subjects in an experiment. What type of a sample is this? What sources of error may have entered into the study?

6. Ask students to give examples of various tests they have taken in school or employment situations. Have them classify the tests as either norm- or criterion-referenced and tell what characteristics of each test led to their classification decision. Describe how the tests were appropriate or inappropriate for the purposes of testing and the particular setting as well as how the results were used.

7. Discuss various types of decisions that would benefit from a regression analysis. Types of decisions might include admission to your department's graduate program in psychology or your college/university undergraduate program and employment decisions. How would the regression analysis be conducted? Differentiate regression from multiple regression. Are more predictors better? Why or why not?

CLASS DEMONSTRATIONS

1. For the data on test scores presented in Table 3–1, calculate class percentile ranks, z scores, and T scores.

2. For the data collected in Demonstration #2 in Chapter 3, compute correlation coefficients between height and weight, height and number of brothers and sisters.

3. As an exercise in correlation, obtain the following data for each student: (1) number of coins (loose change) in pocket or purse, and (2) number of rings on hands. Then (a) draw a scatterplot of the data, and (b) calculate a Pearson r using the computational formula included in the chapter. Does a positive relationship exist? Does an inverse relationship exist? Does *any* relationship exist?

4. Bring in a standardized achievement test report (a non–personally identifiable one can be obtained from your local school district) and make a copy for each of your students. Identify the types of standard scores (e.g., percentiles) that are used and how they enter into the interpretation of the results.

5. Invite one of your college admissions counselors as a guest speaker. Inquire how test scores are used in admissions decisions. What types of norms are used?

6. Huck, Wright, and Park (1992) developed a demonstration of the relationship between spread and the Pearson r. The demonstration is designed to help students understand that increases in standard deviation may lead to an increase or a decrease in r or to no change whatsoever. The exercise uses standard playing cards to generate hypothetical scores on two common variables, IQ and GPA, and students calculate and compare various standard deviations and correlation coefficients.

7. Contact your department's admissions office and bring in a non–personally identifiable set of scores from the GRE. Use this set of scores to illustrate the principles discussed in the chapter's Everyday Psychometrics section, Good Ol' Norms and the GRE. The discussion should focus on the value of fixed reference groups and differences in interpretation using the fixed reference group (reflected in the actual scores) versus the more contemporary norm group (reflected in the percentiles).

SUGGESTED ASSIGNMENTS

1. Have students look through magazines and newspapers and identify products/manufacturers that have made claims about their products based on research and using statistics. The students write or phone the company to obtain more information about the sample used and statistical techniques employed. This exercise is ongoing as students report to the class as they obtain the information. Application to the concepts presented in Chapters 3 and 4 are stressed during discussion (Beins, 1985).

2. Have students contact an admissions counselor at their own and other local colleges/universities. Inquire whether or not local norms are used in choosing score cutoffs for the college admission test.

3. Have students collect data on two continuous variables that are linearly related and ask each to calculate the Pearson r using the computational formula in the chapter. Examples might include height and weight for a sample of students chosen randomly outside the university union. Students can select their own relationships to investigate.

4. Have the students go to the library and conduct a search on one of the psychology data bases such as PSYLIT or ERIC for an example of a meta-analysis. Students should bring the abstract to class to discuss their example.

MEDIA RESOURCES

Statistics at a Glance (1972, U of I, 28 minutes, color). Explains descriptive statistical concepts, such as correlation, in a humorous and entertaining fashion.

Interpreting Test Scores Realistically (1961, PSt, 18 minutes, b&w). Stresses and illustrates the importance of knowing the characteristics of the norm group on which the test scores (percentiles) are based.

Although both of the films listed above are dated, discussion of concepts remain relevant.

REFERENCES

Beins, B. (1985). Teaching the relevance of statistics through consumer-oriented research. *Teaching of Psychology, 12,* 168–169.

Huck, S. W., Wright, S. P., & Park, S. (1992). Pearson's r and spread: A classroom demonstration. *Teaching of Psychology, 19,* 45–47.

Rotton, J., & Kelly, I. W. (1985). Much ado about the full moon: A meta-analysis of lunar-lunacy research. *Psychological Bulletin, 97,* 286–306.

CHAPTER 5

Reliability

The Concept of Reliability
    Sources of Error Variance
        Test construction
        Test administration
        Test scoring and interpretation

Types of Reliability Estimates
    Test-Retest Reliability Estimates
    Parallel Forms and Alternate Forms Reliability Estimates
    Split-Half Reliability Estimates
        The Spearman-Brown formula
    Other Methods of Estimating Internal Consistency
        The Kuder-Richardson formulas
        Coefficient alpha
    Measures of Inter-Scorer Reliability
        The kappa statistic

Using and Interpreting a Coefficient of Reliability
    The Purpose of the Reliability Coefficient
    The Nature of the Test
        Homogeneity versus heterogeneity of test items
        Dynamic versus static characteristics
        Restriction or inflation of range
        Speed versus power tests
        Criterior-referenced tests
    Alternatives to the True Score Model

Reliability and Individual Scores
    The Standard Error of Measurement
    The Standard Error of the Difference Between Two Scores

CLOSE-UP
    The Reliability of the Bayley Scales for Infant Development

EVERYDAY PSYCHOMETRICS
    The Reliability Defense and the Breathalyzer Test

CLASS DISCUSSION QUESTIONS

A simple hypothetical situation might well be enough to spark a lively and thought-provoking discussion on the subject of reliability in measurement. As an example:

> The developers of a new test called the "Willingness to Demonstrate Vulnerability Inventory (WDVI)" administered it to 3,000 Seven-Eleven store managers in the San Francisco area on November 1. For the record, scores on this hypothetical test could theoretically range from 0 to 200 and the mean score for the San Francisco sample was 150 with a standard deviation of 10. On November 30, the same test is readministered to the same 3,000 people; this time, the mean WDVI score is 90 with a standard deviation of 15.

After presenting such a hypothetical situation to the student, questions such as the following may be posed: "What are the factors that would have to be considered in any comprehensive accounting of this occurrence? If you were the developer of this test, what steps would you take next?"

Other potential class discussion questions are as follows:

1. What types of reliability estimates would be appropriate for the following types of tests/ measurements?
   a. typing test (timed)
   b. color blindness
   c. weight from month to month of a 6-week-old infant and a 21-year-old
   d. reading from one week to another
   e. intelligence
   f. mood
   g. weight of melting ice cubes
   h. test of reaction time
   i. your instructor's multiple choice final exam during fall and spring semesters (two different exams)
   j. test of anxiety
   k. essay exam in your English literature course
   l. presidential preference poll
   m. art aptitude test, which includes judging the quality of a clay sculpture
   n. a random sample of students to describing their attitudes toward psychological measurement

2. Why is there a need for different methods of estimating reliability for norm-referenced and criterion-referenced tests?

3. Why does an observed score always represent the combination of the true score plus the error score?

4. Discuss how the standard error of measurement is related to test interpretation.

5. One of your classmates earns an IQ of 100 on a particular intelligence test. Another earns an IQ of 110 on a different test. How is the standard error of the difference score involved in determining whether there exists a difference between the two scores? What factors affect the magnitude of the standard error of the difference score?

6. The following discussion approach relates to the classical true score model of reliability and would likely occur over three class sessions. The approach includes three steps:

   Step I: Sources of Error   After introducing the true score model ($X = T + E$), ask students, using as an example a recent class quiz or exam, where error might originate. Discussion focuses on the hope that the quiz/test score contains some reflection of T. Undoubtedly, however, there is also some error, or E. Just how much E we don't know, and E could have raised or lowered the individual quiz or exam score. Then students are asked what might have caused the test or quiz score to contain some error (E) for them or other students. Most students can think of a number of factors that might have lowered their score, but they are reminded to also come up with factors that might also have raised their scores. As the students identify factors, the instructor groups them (without identifying the groups at first) into the following sets: (1) test construction, including item sampling (from a "domain"); (2) administration (testtaker's attention, motivation, environment, illness, anxiety, and errors the administrator commits); and (3) scoring/interpretation (clerical errors and evaluation of essays or use of formulae).

   After students have finished listing sources of errors, the instructor labels the groups into the ones listed above. It is then noted that all of these factors contribute to E, and E varies for each person taking the test, such that some students have +E, some –E, some large E, and some small E.

   Step 2: Types of Reliability   E is estimated through computing the reliability of the recent quiz or test that was used for discussion purposes. This is accomplished in a variety of ways. The four methods are discussed with the students asked to list and define each. The methods include test-retest reliability, alternate forms reliability, split-half reliability/internal consistency, and inter-rater reliability.

Step 3: Relating Error and Types of Reliability   The students are then divided into groups to discuss the sources of error that each type of reliability is designed to assess, and what sources of error each cannot detect. Each group is assigned one type of reliability. If the class is large enough, it is helpful to break them down into eight groups, and assign the same type of reliability to each of two groups. The groups refer to the lists of sources of error generated in Step 1, organized according to the types of error (construction, administration, scoring/interpretation). Each group is also asked to select a recorder before they begin, who will report back to the rest of the class the results of the group discussion.

After the individual group discussions are completed, the whole class comes back together to discuss the groups' conclusions.

7. Discuss generalizability theory and how it is different from true score theory. List all of the components of true score theory and their equivalent in generalizability theory (e.g., universe score/true score). What are the basic differences in the two theories? Using the hypothetical new test called the "The Willingness to Demonstrate Vulnerability Inventory," referred to above in discussion question #1, create a generalizability study followed by a decision study. Let us assume that this test is being used to choose effective department managers for the store.

8. Relating to the Close-Up in this chapter dealing with the reliability of the Bayley Scales of Infant Development, discuss the students' responses to the question Would they invest in the development of an alternate form of the Bayley if they were the test publisher? Why or why not? Why does the development of an alternate form require a great deal of expense? Discuss why test-retest reliability, using long test-retest time intervals, is inappropriate for tests such as the Bayley. Discuss other types of tests (e.g., state anxiety, mood) for which test-retest might be inappropriate.

CLASS DEMONSTRATIONS

1. Divide students into small groups and ask them to share examples from their testtaking experiences that illustrate various sources of error variance. For example, students can relate situations in which factors (e.g., lighting in the room or noise) affected their performance and therefore contributed to error variance.

2. Divide students into small groups, assign each a method of estimating reliability (e.g., split-half, test-retest), and ask each group to list the advantages and disadvantages of their method. Bring the class back as a whole and ask each group to report a summary of their discussion. You, as the instructor, can tie it together using examples (see discussion question #1).

3. Create a short test measuring knowledge of basic arithmetic operations. The test might include addition, subtraction, multiplication, division, and fraction problems. Administer the test, with a specific time limit, under regular testtaking conditions. Readminister the same test under more adverse conditions such as when you are flashing the lights on and off or playing loud music in the room. Have students exchange papers, or students can score their own. Have students submit (without their names) a piece of paper listing both their scores. Using the group data, compute a rank order (rho) coefficient (see *101 Exercises in Psychological Testing and Assessment, Third Edition,* for a computational formula) that will be the measure of test-retest reliability. It should be lower than expected due to the various sources of error variance introduced.

4. Moore (1981) provides useful suggestions for teaching related reliability concepts such as true score, true variance, and standard error of measurement using measurements of lines. Parallel-forms and inter-scorer reliability are also demonstrated. Requests for reprints can be directed to Dr. Michael Moore, Department of Psychology, University of California, Davis, CA 95616.

5. Buck (1991), using five position, machine-scorable answer sheets and pencils, has created a demonstration of measurement error and reliability. Two answer sheets are prepared as keys for the two forms of the test by randomly choosing one of the answer positions as the correct answer for

each item. Demonstrations of position preference set, chance scores, the relation between chance scores and the standard error of measurement, and the relation between reliability and the standard error of measurement are described in the article.

6. Bring into class a test such as the Peabody Picture Vocabulary Test—Revised, Key Math Diagnostic Test—Revised, or the Woodcock Reading Mastery Test—Revised. Each has alternate forms. Summarize how the alternate forms were developed using information from the technical manuals. For these same tests, or other tests if these are not available, give the class information on the standard error of measurement for the test. Have students calculate scores considering this information. Provide them with particular cutoff scores to make important decisions (e.g., placement in a remedial program) and have them make the decision using the concepts of standard error of measurement and confidence intervals. What level of confidence would they choose and why?

7. Develop a speed test (e.g., letters of the alphabet and students have to record the next letter or alphabetizing a list of words) and administer to the class. Have students calculate a split-half reliability coefficient (see *101 Exercises in Psychological Testing and Assessment, Third Edition*, for a computational formula). Discuss why this type of reliability is inappropriate to use for determining the reliability of a speeded test.

8. Provide the students with two scores on two tests (e.g., scores on a math test and English test) and the standard error of the difference. Ask them to determine if the two scores are different using the concept of standard error of the difference. Discuss the relationship between standard error of measurement and standard error of the difference. Which would be expected to be larger? How is the standard error of the difference calculated? Have students calculate a confidence interval for the difference score.

9. As a follow-up to the chapter section on Everyday Psychometrics dealing with the reliability defense and the breathalyzer test, invite a local town/city or campus police officer to class to discuss the use of breathalyzers by law enforcement agencies. Have students prepare questions in advance dealing with the issue of the different types of reliability that are important to consider for this measure and its implications. Questions can be generated in small groups prior to the arrival of the guest speaker.

SUGGESTED ASSIGNMENTS

1. Students are instructed to check out and review a test manual from their college/university test library and/or look up a test of choice in the *Mental Measurements Yearbook* or *Test Critiques*. They then report on the types of reliability estimates reported for their test of choice. Is the test author's choice of estimate(s) consistent with the information presented in Chapter 5?

2. Ask students to develop an idea for their own test and describe it in a paper. They should include a section relating to the purpose of the test and what it is intended to measure. They should also include what reliability estimates are appropriate and rationale for the ones they choose.

MEDIA RESOURCES

Interpreting Test Scores Realistically (1961, PSt, 18 minutes, b&w). Illustrates the principle of any test score is only an estimate of a student's ability (standard error of measurement).

Standardized Test—An Educational Tool (1962, PSt, 25 minutes, color). Explains and illustrates the concept of error of measurement.

Although both of the above films are dated, the discussion of the concepts presented remains relevant.

REFERENCES

Buck, J. (1991). A demonstration of measurement error and reliability. *Teaching of Psychology, 18,* 46–47.

Moore, M. (1981). An empirical investigation and a classroom demonstration of reliability concepts. *Teaching of Psychology, 8,* 163–164.

CHAPTER 6
Validity

CLASS DISCUSSION QUESTIONS

If your use of our WDVI (Willingness to Demonstrate Vulnerability Inventory) example in the Chapter 5 class discussion was a hit, you may wish to pursue it in this lecture as well. (Alternatively, if the WDVI example went over like a lead balloon, skip down to the questions that follow this paragraph.) To stimulate thought about what is an adequate criterion for demonstrating criterion-related validity, ask students to think of criteria that might be used to validate a test such as the WDVI. And if after that you're still game for pursuing the WDVI for one last example, challenge the students to think about the types of convergent and divergent evidence that might be used to establish the construct validity of the test.

Other potential class discussion questions are as follows:

1. How/why would predictive validity of psychological and/or educational tests be important to people in the following positions:
   a. personnel manager
   b. teacher or principal
   c. college admissions officer
   d. prison warden
   e. psychiatrist
   f. guidance counselor
   g. veterinary dermatologist
   h. professor in medical school

2. What are the advantages and disadvantages of quota systems in employment and academic situations? A panel debate can be organized with one group of students representing the "pro" and another group representing the "con" positions of quota systems. Students can prepare for their debate by reading Hunter and Schmidt (1976) and pages 397–412 of Jensen (1980). As part of their preparation, students can also contact local schools and businesses (personnel directors) to determine if any consideration has been given to a quota system (e.g., enrollment in programs for the gifted).

3. Why is it that face validity is not considered a genuine aspect of validity? Although a test developer cannot use this type of face validity as evidence that the test is valid, why is it important? How might it influence testtakers?

4. What is "blueprinting"? How does it relate to content validity? Explain how you might develop a "blueprint" for your final exam in this measurement course.

5. What are the characteristics of an adequate criterion? Give examples of an adequate criterion to be used for validating your final exam in this course. Will your example measure concurrent or predictive criterion-related validity?

6. Discuss the issue of incremental validity. Have class members come up with some criterion they want to predict and discuss how the concept of incremental validity can be used to increase validity.

7. What is the value of decision theory in employment decision making? What is a base rate? What is a hit, a miss, a false positive, and a false negative? What is a selection ratio? Using the Taylor-Russell table for a base rate of .6 presented in the chapter, give examples that demonstrate that dependent on the selection ratio, even a test with a low validity coefficient can improve decision making. How do the tables developed by Naylor and Shine differ from those developed by Taylor and Russell? What are the limitations of using the Taylor-Russell and Naylor and Shine tables?

8. What is the relationship between construct validity and the other forms of validity evidence?

9. You are a test developer and wish to present only one type of validity for each of the following types of tests to a group of prospective test users at a luncheon. Which would you choose? Why?
   a. mathematics test
   b. intelligence test
   c. vocational interest inventory
   d. music aptitude test
   e. attitude toward school inventory

10. What is test bias? How is it the same or different from the use of the word *bias* in common parlance? From the use of the word *fair* in the professional and lay sense?

11. Discuss situations in which students have been administered tests that they feel were biased and/or unfair.

12. Discuss the relationship between reliability and validity. Can an unreliable test be a valid one? Can a reliable test not have adequate validity? Can a test that has adequate validity be unreliable?

13. A college uses a particular admissions test that possesses adequate predictive validity. However, members of a particular minority group tend to score low on this admissions test. Some students who have been denied admission based on their test scores are criticizing the school for using a biased test. What steps need to be taken prior to making the conclusion the test is biased? What needs to occur to determine if the test is fair to use?

14. If members of one minority group consistently score significantly lower than members of another ethnic group on a particular test, is the test necessarily biased?

15. As a follow-up to the Everyday Psychometrics section of this chapter, have students express their opinions regarding what constitutes a fair use of employment and other tests used in a selection process. Are measurement tools neither the cause of nor the cure for racial inequalities in employment? Solicit student opinions about the use of procedures to adjust test scores on the basis of group membership. Is this legal? Is it ethical? Do students agree with Section 106 of the Civil Rights Act of 1991? Why?

CLASS DEMONSTRATIONS

1. Bring to class the *Standards for Educational and Psychological Testing* to discuss in greater detail different notions of validity.

2. Ask a personnel director and/or school psychologist to speak to your class on the practical implications of the concept of test bias.

3. Write to the Educational Testing Service (Princeton, NJ 08540) and request information relative to the validity including the issue of test bias for the Scholastic Aptitude Test (SAT). Use this information to demonstrate/illustrate concepts presented in Chapter 6.

4. Similar to the federal judges in the Larry P. and PASE cases, students can be divided into two tribunals to hear evidence regarding the issue of bias in mental testing. Evidence can be presented by groups of students assigned to read particular articles referenced in Sattler (1988), and the whole class can view films such as the IQ Myth (see Media Resources section). You, as the instructor, can also be involved in presenting "evidence." At the conclusion of presenting the evidence, the two tribunals meet separately to issue their "decision."

5. Review the WISC/WISC-R items presented in Sattler (1988). Based on the content of each item, poll the students to learn how many believe the item would be more difficult for African-American than for Caucasian children. How many believe it would be easier? Ask the students to provide a rationale for their vote. Discuss this process in relation to what actual panels of "expert" judges do when reviewing items for recently constructed intelligence tests.

6. Choose a recent classroom quiz or exam and divide students up into groups of approximately five students. Ask that each group serve as a panel of "expert judges" and make a determination concerning the content validity of the quiz or exam. Ask them to refer to the section in the chapter dealing with the quantification of content validity. Lead a discussion after the exercise concerning what types of information students used to make their determination and have them calculate a content validity ratio.

7. Divide the class into two groups for a debate on "Should test scores be adjusted on the basis of group membership?" Have the class become more familiar with Section 106 of the Civil Rights Act of 1991.

SUGGESTED ASSIGNMENTS

1. Instruct students to review a test manual from their college/university test library and/or look up a test of choice in the *Mental Measurements Yearbook* or *Test Critiques* and report back on the appropriateness of the validation data reported for their test of choice. Is the test author's choice of methods of validation consistent with the information presented in Chapter 6?

2. Instruct students to review major research journals in an area of interest to them such as clinical (*Psychological Assessment: A Journal of Consulting and Clinical Psychology*), school (*Journal of School Psychology* or *School Psychology Review*), industrial/organizational (*Journal of Personnel Psychology*), educational (*Journal of Educational Psychology*), consumer psychology (*Psychology & Marketing*), or measurement journals such as *Educational and Psychological Measurement*. Ask them to select and summarize a research article reporting the results of a validation study with reference to the information presented in Chapter 6.

3. A group of students can contact the personnel director of a large business or the personnel office of the college or university to inquire whether or not local validation studies are being or have been conducted for any of the tests they are using in employee selection.

4. Have students review a test manual or journal article (in a journal such as *Educational and Psychological Measurement*) in which the results of a factor analysis are presented. Have the students discuss the results as they relate to the information presented in the chapter Close-Up on Factor Analysis and the Correlation Matrix.

MEDIA RESOURCES

The Larry P. Case (1978, INHURTS; INUAV, 30 minutes, color). Film reviews the background, content, and progress of the Larry P. case. Because the production date is 1978, the instructor should supplement with updated material included in the text as well as other sources (see Sattler, 1988).

Selecting an Achievement Test (1961, InU, 14 minutes, b&w). Illustrates the concept of content validity through the demonstration of selecting an achievement test.

Standardized Test—An Educational Tool (1962, PSt, 25 minutes, color). Concept of validity is introduced through a demonstration of a teacher selecting a standardized reading test.

How Can Tests Be Unfair? A Workshop on Nondiscriminatory Testing (Nazzaro, 1975, CEC). A series of simulations illustrating various concepts related to nondiscriminatory testing.

Although resources listed above are dated, illustration and discussion of the concepts presented remain relevant.

REFERENCES

Hunter, J. E., & Schmidt, F. L. (1976). A critical analysis of the statistical and ethical implications of various definitions of "test bias." *Psychological Bulletin, 83,* 1053–1071.

Jensen, A. R. (1980). *Bias in mental testing.* New York: The Free Press.

Nazzaro, J. N. (1975). *How can tests be unfair? A workshop on nondiscriminatory testing.* Reston, VA: Council for Exceptional Children.

Sattler, J. M. (1988). *Assessment of children.* (3d Ed.). San Diego, CA: Jerome Sattler Publisher.

CHAPTER 7
Test Development

CLASS DISCUSSION QUESTIONS

As stated in the chapter, the beginnings of any published test can probably be traced to thoughts—"self-talk" in behavioral terms. The test developer says to himself or herself something like "There ought to be a test designed to measure *(fill in the blank)* in *(such and such)* way."

It would seem that a convenient point of departure for a lecture on test development would be the *students'* self-talk in this context. What kind of a psychological test do they feel needs to be developed? After specifying the content area and considering the process of test conceptualization, have students consider in detail each of the remaining elements in the test development process including test construction, test tryout, analysis of findings, test revision, and so forth.

Other potential class discussion questions are as follows:

1. What are the advantages and disadvantages of the different types of test item formats (multiple choice, matching, true/false, short answer, completion, and essay)? Encourage students to share their experiences and reactions to each type of item (e.g., Which item type do they prefer and why?).

2. What factors should be considered when an instructor is deciding how to grade a particular test?

3. For the Attitudes Toward Statistics Scale presented in Chapter 3, discuss the concepts presented regarding scaling. What type of scale is it? What methods might have been used in constructing this scale?

4. Give examples (drawn from the text and/or your own experience or that of your colleagues who may use rating scales) of various types of rating scales (Guttman, categorical scaling, sorting tasks, equal appearing intervals, etc.) and classify each.

CLASS DEMONSTRATIONS

1. Using the material presented in the *K-ABC Interpretive Manual* (Kaufman & Kaufman, 1983), present to the class each of the five stages of test development for the K-ABC. These stages and their corresponding page numbers in the K-ABC manual include test conceptualization and test construction (p. 59), test tryout (pp. 59–60), item analysis (pp. 60–62), and test revision (pp. 63–64). If the K-ABC is unavailable, choose another test from your test library.

2. Arrange for a guest speaker from a local school district or the personnel director of a local business to discuss the employee rating forms they use and how they were developed. Alternatively, share the teacher/instructor evaluation forms used in your own department for evaluation purposes and critique them. Classify the rating scale as to type and discuss how it was developed.

3. If your local school district uses a minimal competency examination, a district representative can be invited to class to share the steps taken to develop, design, and implement the use of the exam. In a follow-up written assignment, students can critique the test development methods discussed by the guest speaker with those presented in the chapter.

4. Relating to the chapter's Everyday Psychometrics section, bring to class a copy of the last exam (or last year's final examination) including the computerized item analysis results. Ask the class how the test might be evaluated from a psychometric point of view. Refer the students to the chapter's Everyday Psychometrics section and parts of the chapter relating to what makes a good item. Select several items for the students to evaluate. Based on the guidelines presented in the chapter and focusing only on how the items are written, have students rate each item as "well written" or "poorly written." Discussion can then focus on how one can use the computerized item analysis results to identify "good" and "bad" items. What type of scoring system (cumulative, class, or ipsative) was used? Now compare the judgments of the students as to which items were well written or poorly written with the actual item analysis data. If the conclusions are consistent, what does this suggest about the item? How might the test be made more psychometrically sound? How might particular items be improved? In order for more students to become actively involved in the discussion, groups can be formed and test items divided up with the same item given to at least two groups in order to compare their decisions.

5. Using a recent classroom test, use one of the qualitative methods of item analysis described in the text such as an interview (see Table 7–2) or "think aloud." Discuss the advantages/disadvantages of this approach.

SUGGESTED ASSIGNMENTS

1. Using the concepts presented in Chapter 7, have the students write 20 to 30 questions covering material presented in this chapter. Students might also be divided into groups. The questions should include a certain number of multiple choice (with three or four foils per item) and a certain number of matching, true-false, short answer, sentence completion, and one or two essay questions. The students must also provide the correct answers for each question. You might then use the best items from each student/group as part of the next exam that covers this chapter. The instructor would also run an item analysis for each question and share the results with the class.

2. Have the students work in small groups of three or four to develop an item pool of 40 statements to include in a 20-item "self-concept" scale. The group must choose what type of scaling method they will use and what the forced-choice responses will be.

3. Using the interview approach (see Table 7–2) described in the chapter, have students interview each other concerning their last classroom exam. To be most relevant, the interviews should occur immediately after completing the exam.

4. Have students read the article "How a Standardized Achievement Test Is Built" (Test Service Notebook #125 published by the Psychological Corporation and reprinted in *101 Exercises in Psychological Testing and Assessment, Third Edition*). It can serve as a useful stimulus to discuss further issues related to test development.

MEDIA RESOURCES

Making Your Own Tests (1960, ETS, 2LP331/3 records, color). Kit that includes three filmstrips, long-playing records, and a work kit that presents and illustrates concepts related to planning a classroom test, constructing items, and analyzing test results.

One in a Hundred (1966, ETS, 25 minutes, b&w). Describes how the Educational Testing Service (ETS) constructs a test. Film depicts construction of one item in the hundred to be included in the College Board Achievement test in American History and Social Studies.

Tests, Tests, Tests (1982, InU, 11 minutes, color). Presents concepts related to the development of standardized tests such at the Cognitive Abilities Test (CAT), Scholastic Aptitude Test (SAT), and the American College Testing Program (ACT).

Although some of the resources listed above appear dated, the discussion of the concepts illustrated remains relevant.

REFERENCE

Kaufman, A. S. & Kaufman, N. L. (1983). *Kaufman assessment battery for children (K-ABC) interpretive manual*. Circle Pines, MN: American Guidance Service.

PART 3
THE ASSESSMENT OF INTELLIGENCE

CHAPTER 8
Intelligence and Its Measurement

CLASS DISCUSSION QUESTIONS

Alfred Binet developed his test in response to the Paris school board's request for a method of identifying "slow" children. This scenario could be reenacted at the front of the class by two student volunteers (or two students "volunteered" by the professor). One student plays the role of the head of the school board, the other the role of the psychological assessor asked to develop an instrument to identify children who might require and profit from a special education program. Have other class members act as participant/observers in the discussion—raising questions, comments, or issues on the topics such as the nature of intelligence, what intelligence tests should measure, and so forth. Note that you may wish to resume this type of exercise in your lecture material for Chapter 16 (where you might additionally wish the students to focus on the issues attendant to special class placement).

Another jumping-off point for discussion relates to a request, early in the chapter, by the authors for the readers to take out a sheet of paper and jot down their own definitions of the word "intelligence." They are then asked to compare their definitions to the many different ones that appear in the chapter. Discussion can focus on the students' definitions of intelligence.

Still another jumping-off point for this chapter, which is filled with potentially stimulating issues for class discussion, relates to the issues raised in the Everyday Psychometrics section of the chapter, *The Bell Curve* Controversy. Students can be asked to react to the conclusions and recommendations of the authors of the book that are summarized in this section.

Other potential class discussion questions are as follows:

1. How were Binet's ideas ahead of his time? What aspects of Binet's views are still evident in theory and practice today? What aspects of his ideas are no longer supported by modern-day psychologists?

2. Compare and contrast the conceptions intelligence advanced by Binet, Wechsler, Piaget, Galton, Spearman, Naglieri et al., and Sternberg.

3. "Any interesting personal experiences with intelligence tests you'd like to share with the class?" Incorporate responses, if any, into the lecture material.

4. Give various examples of successive and simultaneous information processing. For example:
   a. Giving the following directions: "Go up to the stop sign, turn right, go three blocks and turn left." (successive)
   b. A master chef who needs no recipes (simultaneous)
   c. Reading comprehension (simultaneous)
   d. Mastering math facts (successive)
   e. Understanding proverbs (simultaneous)

5. A great deal of the discussion in this chapter explores the multifaceted aspects of the heredity/environment question regarding measured intelligence. Discussion can focus on the exploration of students' views, opinions, and beliefs both prior and subsequent to reading this chapter. A simple question such as the one posed in the text—"Do you believe that intellectual ability is innate and that it simply 'unfolds' from birth onward?"—may be enough to stimulate a very lively and ultimately informative class discussion.

6. What do the terms *performationism* and *predeterminism* mean? What are the subtle differences in the meanings of the two terms?

7. What behaviors of children and/or adults would support a predeterministic philosophy (e.g., walking, early stages of speech/language development—even babies that are born deaf babble, etc.)?

8. How did Gesell's work influence his predeterministic viewpoint? How might such a viewpoint influence an interpretation of infant intelligence test data? How might it affect recommendations for intervention if you should diagnose an infant who was significantly developmentally delayed or advanced?

9. What is the interactionist viewpoint of the development of intelligence? How might this viewpoint affect your interpretation of infant intelligence tests and recommendations for intervention?

10. What is the nature of the relationship between age and the stability of intelligence test scores? What factors account for this observed relationship? How might your knowledge of this relationship affect your interpretations of intelligence-test scores and recommendations?

11. In Chapter 8 is the statement that " . . . females as a group tend to score slightly higher than males as a group in tasks involving verbal ability, while males tend to outscore females in tasks involving quantitative or mathematical ability" even though these differences are not statistically significant. Discuss the arguments that could account for these observed differences based on environmental (social and cultural factors) and predeterministic viewpoints.

12. Compare and contrast the concepts culture-free, culture-fair, culture-specific, culture-loading, and culture-reduced. Apply them to the following questions that might appear on the Information subtest of one or more of the Wechsler scales:
    a. Who is vice-president of the United States?
    b. How many are three and four marbles?
    c. Sample items from the Culture Fair Test of Intelligence.
    d. Items from the Black Intelligence Test of Cultural Homogeneity
    f. Items from the CRUST Test.

13. What factors may account for the fact that African-Americans tend to score lower than Caucasians on nonverbal and verbal tests (e.g., cultural difference, cultural deprivation, inability to understand written or oral directions, lack of interest/motivation in the testing situation, and other personality factors)?

14. Why might Martin Kallikak's offspring by the "mentally defective waitress" be "far less socially desirable" than his "legitimate" children with his wife who had normal intelligence? What explanation was offered by Goddard? What alternative explanations might be advanced (educational opportunity, societal expectations, cultural differences, child-rearing, modeling, poor nutrition, personality factors, lack of environmental stimulation, etc.)?

15. What is the relationship between prevailing attitudes relative to the nature-nurture issue of cognitive development and social-policy decisions such as infant and preschool educational programs (e.g., Headstart) and affirmative action programs in education and business? Identify other social-policy decisions by government and business that could be influenced by the prevailing thoughts on this issue. How do Hernstein and Murray in their book, *The Bell Curve: Intelligence and Class Structure in American Life*, respond to these issues?

16. Are slang terms such as those that appear on tests like the BITCH universally accepted across all African-American cultures and across time?

17. Compare and contrast the findings/themes that emerged related to the definition of intelligence from the 1921 Symposium and more recent discussions in 1986.

CLASS DEMONSTRATIONS

1. Invite a school psychologist from your local school district to speak on the topic of which conception(s) of intelligence has been found to be most useful for work in identifying exceptional individuals in the schools.

2. Prior to the students reading Chapter 8, have each one write down a description of the behaviors associated with academic intelligence, everyday intelligence, intelligence, and unintelligence. The instructor can then list the students' responses on a class handout as a stimulus for class discussion. The class can also assess the similarity and differences of their responses as well as comparing them to the results of the study by Sternberg described in the chapter.

At the conclusion of Part 3, ask the students to again write down their own definitions/conceptions of intelligence to determine if their views have changed as a result of what they have learned about intelligence.

3. Invite a psychologist who works with infants and the elderly to speak on the types of cognitive tests he or she uses and their purpose in assessment.

4. Obtain complete copies of the BITCH (Williams, 1975), the CRUST (Herlihy, 1977), and the Culture Fair Test of Intelligence (Cattell, 1940). Administer them to the class as a whole. Discuss the class's reactions and address the issues presented in Chapter 8 (i.e., how culture affects measured intelligence). Ask students what types of items they might add so that the test would measure judgment, abstraction, problem-solving ability, memory, and other cognitive skills related to a more comprehensive definition of intelligence.

5. Invite as a guest speaker a clinical or developmental psychologist who specializes in gerontology and has experience assessing the intelligence of people over age 65. Ask the guest speaker to address the issues presented in the section of the "Rise and Fall of IQ."

6. Invite as a guest speaker a developmental psychologist or specialist in the areas of the gifted who could lecture more extensively on the genetic and environmental factors associated with high measured intelligence.

7. Utilize with your class the simulations included in *How Tests Can Be Unfair? A Workshop on Nondiscriminatory Testing* (Nazzara, 1975).

8. Invite a clinical psychologist to class to discuss the impact of psychological disorders on measured intelligence.

SUGGESTED ASSIGNMENTS

1. Have the students write a paper or prepare for an oral presentation concerning the theorist or theory of intelligence that has the most appeal to them. They should be very specific in justifying their reasons why they believe that the particular theory or theorist they have chosen is the most satisfactory one for conceptualizing intelligence. If you elect the oral presentation option, it could be made into a political debate format with time limits for defending their theory of choice and time limits for rebuttals. For example, "We will now hear from Guilford, who will have three minutes to persuasively present his conception of intelligence." Students can then take a vote to determine if there exists any consensus on the definition of intelligence after the debate.

2. Provide copies of Jensen's (1969) article published in the *Harvard Educational Review* to all members of the class, and have students prepare a written summary and critique. Students can also be assigned to read excerpts from *The Bell Curve: Intelligence and Class Structure in American Life*, and have students prepare a written summary and critique. Class discussion could then focus on their reactions to the two pieces and around their similarities and differences.

3. Have class members prepare a list and research famous individuals such as Michael Jordan, Albert Einstein, Thomas Edison, Bill Clinton, etc. The assignment is to list the various factors that might account for their superior achievement in their chosen field (e.g., music, athletics, politics, etc.) and to classify the factors as supporting the "nature" or "nurture" position.

4. Divide the class up into two groups, the "nature" view of intellectual development and the "nurture" position. The groups would be required to research their positions culminating in a class debate on the nature/nurture issue. After the debate, the two groups might discuss whether or not they would be willing to support the interactionist point of view as a compromise position.

MEDIA RESOURCES

Aspects of Intelligence: The Growing Years Series (RMI, 30 minutes, b&w). This lesson deals with intelligence and its measurement.

Cognitive Development: Human Development: First Two and One Half Years Series (1991, CM, 25 minutes, color, VHS). Describes child's sensory-motor stage of cognitive development.

Cognitive Development (1992, CM, 28 minutes, color). Describes Piaget's theories regarding cognitive development including the processes of assimilation and accommodation. Discusses preoperational thought including concepts such as irreversibility, static thought, egocentrism, conservation, classification, magical thought, animism, and ritualistic behavior. Discusses language development and includes section on facilitating cognitive development.

Developing Psychometry Skills (AAVP, 53 minutes, b&w video). Addresses the measurement of intelligence, aptitude, and emotions. Demonstrates the necessary steps involved in developing psychometry skills.

Development of Individual Differences (1957, McH, 21 minutes, b&w). Discusses the issue of the relative contribution of heredity and environment on behavior using as an example the behavior of two brothers from one family compared to an only child raised in another family.

Growth of Intelligence in the Preschool Years (1989, ISN, 31 minutes). Children from infancy to six years of age perform tasks designed by Jean Piaget and his collaborators. These tasks reveal how intellectual thought develops and manifests itself in early childhood.

How Can Tests Be Unfair? A Workshop on Nondiscriminatory Testing (Nazzaro, 1975). A series of simulations illustrating various concepts related to nondiscriminatory testing including culture-specific tests.

Intelligence: A Complex Concept (1978, IU, 28 minutes, color). Presents the numerous ideas about the nature of intelligence including interviews with people on the street. The more formal conceptions of Piaget and J. P. Guilford are also presented.

IQ Myth (1975, IU, 51 minutes, color/b&w). Presents a critical examination of the validity of the IQ test. Originally presented as part of the *CBS Reports* series.

The IQ Myth (Sir Cyril Burt Controversy) (1977, IU, 15 minutes, color). Discusses the controversy surrounding the discovery that much of the research by Sir Cyril Burt on genetic transference of intelligence was faked. Mike Wallace of *CBS News* conducts a series of interviews with those critical of Burt and his theory as well as those who still support his conclusions.

Piaget's Developmental Theory (1989, PSt, 17–45 minutes, color, film or VHS). Series of five films illustrating Piaget's stages on the cognitive development of children. Film I Classification (1969, 17 minutes) illustrates children performing such mental operations as multiple classification, class inclusion, and hierarchical classification. Film II (1969, 28 minutes) demonstrates conservation tasks of quantity, length, area, and volume. Film III Formal Thought (1971, 32 minutes) illustrates formal thought in secondary school students. Film IV Memory and Film V The Growth of Intelligence in the Preschool Years (1972, 30 minutes) illustrates the growth of the thinking process in the preschool years.

Piaget's Developmental Theory: An Overview (1989, DF, 27 minutes, color). The film presents an overview of Piaget's work, dividing it into four periods. Dr. David Elkind conducts interviews with children of various ages.

Race, Intelligence, and Education (1974, PSt, 53 minutes, color). Introduces Professor H. J. Eysenck and his theory that heredity influences intellectual development more than environment. Six other scientists are also interviewed and react to this theory and others.

REFERENCES

Cattell, R. B. (1940). A Culture-Free Intelligence Test. *Journal of Educational Psychology, 31,* 161–179.

Herlihy, B. (1977). Watch out, IQ myth: Here comes another debunker. *Phi Delta Kappan, 59,* 298.

Jensen, A. R. (1969). How much can we boost IQ and scholastic achievement? *Harvard Educational Review, 39,* 1–123.

Nazzaro, J. N. (1975). *How can tests be unfair? A workshop on nondiscriminatory testing.* Reston, VA: Council for Exceptional Children.

Williams, R. (1975). The BITCH-100: A culture-specific test. *Journal of Afro-American Issues, 3,* 103–116.

CHAPTER 9

Tests of Intelligence

CLASS DISCUSSION QUESTIONS

The introductory material for this chapter in the text reads, in part, as follows:

> As you read about these tests, contemplate how the types of tasks on them fit into your own conception of what intelligence is and how it can best be measured. For example, how does the conception of intelligence that guided the authors of the Stanford-Binet Fourth Edition or the Wechsler series fit with your own conceptions of what intelligence is and how it can best be measured?

Other potential class discussion questions are as follows:

1. Discuss the strengths and relative weaknesses of the most recent edition of the Stanford-Binet Intelligence Scale.

2. What are the features common to all the Wechsler scales? What are their strengths? Identify their limitations.

3. Why is the vocabulary subtest generally viewed as the best single measure of general intelligence?

4. What similarities and differences exist between the Stanford-Binet Fourth Edition and the Wechsler scales?

5. What are the advantages of having a test that yields Verbal, Performance, and Full Scale scores?

6. Discuss the advantages and limitations of administering intelligence tests in groups. What are the advantages of group over individual tests? For what purposes are group tests recommended? For what purposes should they never be used?

7. If you were a testing coordinator for a school district, what would you include in a policy to help to ensure that group test results are used in a maximally effective and appropriate manner?

8. If any students have taken any group test administered by the military, ask if they would share their recollections of the content of the test and how the results were used.

9. Why are restandardizations of tests—intelligence as well as others—necessary?

10. Why is a behavioral observation during an individually administered intelligence test so important?

11. Discuss the pros and cons of using figure drawings for the assessment of intelligence. Cite the reliability and validity data presented in the chapter to support your conclusions.

12. As a follow-up to the chapter's Everyday Psychometrics section, discuss the advantages and disadvantages of adaptive testing and its application to consumer assessment and marketing, intelligence testing, behavioral assessment, and measurement of personality and attitudes and values.

13. As a follow-up to the chapter Close-Up on Construct Validity, Factor Analysis, and the WISC-III, review the WISC-III factor analytic data presented in the Close-Up and discuss how these data contribute to the validation of the WISC-III. Review a particular theorist (Spearman, Binet, Wechsler, etc.) presented in Chapter 8 and have students predict the results of the factor analysis that would be necessary to contribute to the validation of the tests based on these theories of intelligence.

CLASS DEMONSTRATIONS

1. The instructor or an appropriately trained colleague might administer parts of the WISC-III or WPPSI-R and the Stanford-Binet Fourth Edition to a student in the class in a role-playing situation or to an actual child. For test security purposes, the WAIS-R and the upper limits of the Stanford-Binet Fourth Edition should not be used for demonstration in an undergraduate class nor should the complete scales be administered. Rather, the objective of this demonstration is only to give your students a better understanding of the various types of cognitive abilities that are assessed on this scale and as a supplement to the information presented in the chapter. If a live demonstration is not possible, one of the media resources listed below can be used for this purpose.

2. The instructor could bring to class and demonstrate the use of the Slosson Intelligence Test—Revised. The subsequent discussion could highlight the limitations of this instrument.

3. A practicing school or clinical psychologist could be invited to class as a guest speaker to discuss his/her experiences with the tests discussed in Chapter 9. From a personal viewpoint, the individual can discuss the advantages and disadvantages of the available tests of intelligence as well as their uses and misuses. Additionally, the importance of behavioral observations while testing may be discussed.

4. The instructor can bring in for discussion a computerized printout from a scoring and/or interpretation software program for one of the Wechsler scales, Stanford-Binet, or another test discussed in Chapter 9. A possible source of this information would be the on-campus psychology clinic, the student counseling center, or a faculty colleague who either teaches or uses these tests in clinical work with adults or children.

5. As a class, students can be administered a Draw-A-Person to assess intellectual functioning. Based on the instructor's own knowledge or after consulting with a knowledgeable colleague, characteristics of the figures and the number of points they would earn can be discussed. Based on this experience, discuss the limitations of using this approach to assess intelligence. What factors contribute to lowered reliability and validity of the test? For what purposes would members of the class recommend this test of intelligence?

SUGGESTED ASSIGNMENTS

1. Assign your students to research journal articles that report on validity studies of the three Wechsler scales. They could then prepare a written report summarizing the study (including a critique) and/or prepare an oral report of the study for presentation to classmates. The same assignment can be given for the Stanford-Binet Fourth Edition.

2. Students can administer a nonrestricted test such as the Slosson to a child of a neighbor or friend and report back to the class.

3. Students can be assigned to look up various test reviews of the Stanford-Binet Intelligence Scale in current and prior editions of the *Mental Measurements Yearbook* and *Test Critiques*. Class discussion can focus on similarities and differences in the reviews and relating the reviewer's comments to what is presented in Chapter 9.

4. Assign groups of students one of the tests discussed in Chapter 9. The group is instructed to look up the test in the most recent *Mental Measurements Yearbook* or *Test Critiques* and summarize in writing the comments made by the test reviewers. Also in their written report, the students can compare and contrast the different reviewers' conclusions.

MEDIA RESOURCES

Aspects of Individual Mental Testing (1960, PSt, 33 minutes, b&w). Describes and illustrates items used in different phases of testing with the 1937 revision of the Stanford-Binet. Can be used to supplement the section in the text dealing with the historical development of the Stanford-Binet as well as illustrating some of the item types that are found in the test.

Fourth Edition of the Stanford-Binet Intelligence Scale (1985, RivP, 30 minutes, color, VHS). Presents an overview with one of the Fourth Edition authors, Robert Thorndike, who discusses the theory on which the test is based and the major distinguishing characteristics of the *Fourth Edition*. Jerome Sattler, another test author, demonstrates some of the specific subtests included in this edition of the test.

Good Testing Procedures (1982, AIC, 17 minutes, color, VHS). Utilizing an actual administration of the WISC-R, demonstrates important issues related to establishing rapport, dealing with frustration, setup and handling of materials, maintaining motivation, observation of test behavior, and many other typical situations.

Intelligence: A Complex Concept (1978, IU, 28 minutes, color). Presents the numerous ideas about the nature of intelligence including interviews with people on the street. The more formal conceptions of Piaget and J. P. Guilford are also presented.

Intelligence Testing of Tom (1961, NSYU, 52 minutes, b&w). Illustrates the use of the Wechsler Intelligence Scale for Children with an exceptionally gifted youngster (previously scored 196 on an earlier edition of the Stanford-Binet).

No Two Alike (1962, U of MN, 30 minutes, b&w). Dr. Lloyd Humphries discusses how tests were developed for selecting pilots during WWII. Dr. James Gallagher demonstrates methods being used to develop creative thinking in the classroom.

The WISC-R: An Overview (1982, AIC, 27 minutes, color, VHS). Brief introduction to the uses and structure of the Wechsler Intelligence Scale for Children—Revised. Uses samples of the content of the actual WISC-R subtests and demonstrates administration.

CHAPTER 10
Preschool and Educational Assessment

Preschool Assessment
    Preschool Tests

Achievement Tests
    Measures of General Achievement
    Measures of Achievement in Specific Subject Areas

Test of Aptitude
    The Elementary School Level
        The Metropolitan Readiness Tests (MRT)
    The Secondary School Level
        The Scholastic Aptitude Test (SAT)
    The College Level and Beyond

Diagnostic Tests
    Reading Tests
        The Woodcock Reading Mastery Tests—Revised
    Math Tests
    Other Diagnostic Tests
    Learning Disabilities Assessment

Psychoeducational Test Batteries
    Kaufman Assessment Battery for Children (K-ABC)
        The standardization sample
        Psychometric properties
        Administering the test
        Scoring and interpreting the test
        An evaluation

Other Tests Used in Educational Settings
    The Peabody Picture Vocabulary Test—Revised (PPVT-R)
    Peer Appraisal Techniques
    Performance, Portfolio, and Authentic Assessment
    Study Habits, Interests, and Attitudes

CLOSE-UP
    Tests of Minimum Competency

EVERYDAY PSYCHOMETRICS
    Adapting to Adaptive Testing: The Case of the GRE

CLASS DISCUSSION QUESTIONS

In this chapter a distinction is made between the terms *achievement* and *aptitude*. How do students feel about this distinction; does it agree with the conception they have of these terms? How do these terms differ in meaning from related terms such as *intelligence?* Do students agree with some experts that the words *intelligence* and *aptitude* are synonymous? These are some of the questions that may be useful in generating a discussion of tests used in an educational context.

Other potential class discussion questions are as follows:

1. Discuss the implications of the stability and predictive validity research on preschool tests of intelligence.

2. Compare and contrast the assessment of intelligence in infancy with that at the preschool and school-age levels. What challenges are faced by the assessor who works with children at these very young ages?

3. Discuss the reasons why the results of infant tests of intelligence typically do not correspond well to the results yielded by intelligence tests when the child reaches school age. What factors likely impact these validity coefficients?

4. Discuss the concept of the at-risk child. If infant and preschool tests of intelligence have little predictive value, what (if anything) is their value?

5. Discuss the differentiation of diagnosis from screening.

6. If you were to develop your own infant and preschool scale, what would it include? What would the materials look like?

7. Have you (students) ever taken an advanced placement test? Describe your experience.

8. React to the findings reported in Figure 10–2, The World (of test items) According to Students.

9. Ask foreign students to discuss their experiences with tests of English proficiency (see Table 10–4 listing various tests of English proficiency). Which test was administered? How were the results used?

10. What is the difference between tests of aptitude and tests of achievement?

11. Should merit pay be issued to teachers based in part on their students' achievement test scores? Given your knowledge of achievement tests, what are your views of this proposal? Take the perspective of the taxpayer, parent, teacher, and school administrator in answering this question.

12. Discuss the theory on which the K-ABC was developed. Compare and contrast the K-ABC with the Woodcock-Johnson Psycho-Educational Battery—Revised (WJ-R) and other tests reviewed in the chapters on intelligence testing. Compare and contrast the definitions of intelligence used and the interpretive approaches utilized in the psychoeducational test batteries presented in the chapter. Compare and contrast the technical strengths and weaknesses of these instruments (i.e., standardization samples, reliability, and validity evidence). Comment on the validity evidence for the teaching strategies based on K-ABC "processing strengths." Discuss how the batteries compare in terms of "culture fairness."

13. After reading the section on college aptitude tests, what are your reactions to them? Do you feel the confidence placed in them by college admissions committees is justified?

14. What is a learning disability? How is the condition diagnosed? What are the problems inherent in the definition? Discuss the various methods of identifying specific learning disabilities with a particular focus on discrepancy formulas.

15. Discuss the pros and cons of minimal competency exams.

16. Why can't the PPVT-R be considered a test of general intelligence? For what purposes can the PPVT-R be used? How can it be useful with individuals with disabilities?

17. Are you a "sequential" or "simultaneous" learner? Why? How might a teacher use this type of information to develop teaching strategies to use in the classroom?

18. Refer back to the discussion of anchor norms and the GRE in the Everyday Psychometrics section of Chapter 4. Compare and contrast this concept with the information provided on the SAT in Chapter 10. Discuss similarities and differences between the norm groups of the GRE and SAT.

19. As a follow-up to the chapter's Everyday Psychometrics section on Adapting to Adaptive Testing: The Case of the GRE, discuss the advantages and disadvantages of the computerized version of the GRE. What special problems did it cause? Compare and contrast the concept of adaptive testing on the GRE, Stanford-Binet Fourth Edition, and the K-ABC. Has any student in this class taken the computerized version of the GRE? If so, what were their reactions?

20. Discuss the advantages and disadvantages of portfolio and authentic assessment.

CLASS DEMONSTRATIONS

1. A guest speaker from a local hospital neonatal or an agency infant-stimulation program (e.g., local Association for Retarded Citizens) can be invited to class to discuss the use of infant scales of intelligence in their work. What types of tests are used with this age group? What do they perceive to be their advantages and limitations?

2. A school psychologist working in a preschool setting can be invited to class to discuss the topic of psychological assessment of preschoolers. The focus of the talk should be on the purpose of assessment (screening or diagnosis versus program planning) and the types of approaches used.

3. A developmental psychologist specializing in infancy can be invited to class to speak about the development and assessment of cognition in infancy.

4. Locate a representative from your local school district to discuss the types of preschool screening procedures used in their district. Compare and contrast it with the types of procedures presented in the chapter.

5. Bring in for demonstration purposes one or more of the tests discussed in this chapter such as a reading test.

6. A school psychologist and a guidance counselor or director of testing from your local school system could be invited to class as guest speakers to discuss the use of tests in the educational setting. The school psychologist might address the use of individually administered tests while the guidance counselor or director of testing could discuss the use of group tests. Achievement, aptitude, and readiness tests used at the different levels can be discussed. Other topics that might be addressed include (1) how the tests are administered, (2) how results are used, and (3) how the results are communicated to parents (see readings in the *101 Exercises in Psychological Testing and Assessment, Third Edition*, "On Telling Parents about Test Results" and "Some Things Parents Should Know About Testing"). Also, have the guests address the issue of whether or not group tests are administered to all children in the district (including those enrolled in special education classes).

7. Another guest speaker could be a college/university admissions officer who would discuss the use of the SAT and ACT and other factors in the admissions process used at their institution. This guest speaker might also be able to address the recent changes in the SAT. As the instructor for this course, you might also want to write to the College Board to get an update on the implementation of these changes to integrate with your lectures. In addition, a representative of the graduate school could speak regarding the use of the GRE and the Millers Analogies Test in admissions decisions for the graduate school.

8. A special education administrator or school psychologist could be invited to class to discuss issues related to the identification of children with learning disabilities in their district. How are they identified? How is the severe discrepancy determined between ability and achievement? Are any modifications made in the administration of group tests for students with disabilities?

9. Various methods of peer appraisal are discussed in the chapter such as the "Guess Who" and nomination, and these can be demonstrated in the class. A sociogram can then be developed. Subsequent discussion can focus on the advantages and limitations of this approach for gathering assessment data.

10. Groups of students can contact school districts in the surrounding area to determine if they use minimal competency examinations (and if so their rationale for using). The content of the exam as well as related psychometric issues and test development methods can also be addressed. The information gained from the students' interviews can be shared with the class as a whole.

11. The instructor can bring to class copies of *Practicing to Take the GRE Psychology Test,* or show in class *The GRE Video Review* (see Media Resources section) as a stimulus to discuss the varied issues touched on therein (such as the issue of coaching).

12. Someone on your faculty in the psychology department or special education departments or a representative from a local school district could administer parts of the K-ABC or Woodcock-Johnson to members of the class role-playing school-age children.

SUGGESTED ASSIGNMENTS

1. A great deal of debate currently exists concerning the reliability and validity of preschool screening tests. Some have argued that they should be declared illegal, as they are discriminatory and may serve to keep children out of school. The class can be divided into two groups. One group would be given the pro screening position and the other the con position.

2. Each student chooses one of the preschool assessment methods presented in Table 10–1 and/or one of the achievement tests listed in Tables 10–2 or 10–3. Students are asked to locate and summarize in writing current reviews of their test in reference books such as the *Mental Measurements Yearbook* or *Test Critiques.*

3. Assign groups of students to contact and interview appropriate personnel working in settings such as the local schools, large businesses, and government offices to determine what types of achievement and/or aptitude tests are used and for what purposes.

4. Divide students into two groups. One group would research and represent the pro side of minimal competency exams, and the other group would represent the con position. To support their particular position, the students could review the relevant literature including those mentioned in the chapter Close-Up, or interview public school administrators, teachers, students, parents, business/ community leaders, and school board members. After the research is completed, an in-class debate could be held.

5. To illustrate the Peer Appraisal Techniques discussed in the chapter, questions using the "Guess Who" format can actually be administered to the class and a sociogram developed.

6. Divide students into groups and have them grapple with how they would utilize portfolio and authentic assessment for the course for which they are using this text. How would they demonstrate the reliability and validity of each form of assessment? What types of reliability and validity evidence would be most appropriate? Each group appoints a recorder who reports back to the large group at the end of the class period.

MEDIA RESOURCES

ABCs of School Testing (1994, NCME, 30 minutes, color video). Explains basics of testing in the school setting. Developed for parents but provides good introduction to basic issues in testing and assessment. Includes a leader's guide.

ABCs of Specific Learning Disabilities (1984, MOU, 45 minutes, color, VHS). Illustrates and demonstrates the various characteristics of specific learning disabilities. Includes group simulations of the various types and discusses their impact on the learning process.

Administration of the Illinois Test of Psycholinguistic Abilities—ITPA (1969, IU, 43 minutes, b&w). Demonstration of the ITPA is made through the actual testing of a six-year-old boy. One of the examiners is Samuel Kirk, the educator who coined the term "learning disabilities." Although the ITPA has been criticized for its lack of technical adequacy and for this reason is not reviewed in the text, the instructor may want to use the film to supplement a lecture related to the historical development of the field. In addition, for many years, the ITPA was the most frequently used assessment instrument for the diagnosis of learning disabilities. This is no longer the case and discussion can focus on the psychometric inadequacies of the test and how this contributed to its recent disuse.

Assessment and the Early Years (1993, JF, 21 minutes, color, VHS). Part of the Fetal Alcohol Syndrome Series Part 3, the video examines the role of diagnosis and assessment in caring for a child with Fetal Alcohol Syndrome.

Be Prepared for the ACT (1983, UMN, 30 minutes, color). Discusses types of effective strategies students can use in responding to questions of the ACT.

Diagnosis—Formal and Informal (1969, ICarbs, 15 minutes, color). Demonstrates ways that the reading ability of pupils can be diagnosed thorough the use of formal and informal diagnostic tests. Illustrates test selection, administration, and interpretation.

The Evaluation by the School Psychologist (1977, PSt, 20 minutes, color). Demonstrates the evaluation of a student referred for possible learning disabilities. Includes diagnostic testing, parent conference to discuss the findings, plan remediation, and suggested ways the parents can assist. Explanation of the concepts of visual and auditory perception problems is also presented.

The GRE Video Review (1987, CAM 3, 2 hours, VHS). Provides an overview of the Verbal, Quantitative, and Analytic sections of the GRE and provides examples of testtaking strategies.

Individual Differences: Infancy to Early Childhood (1978, PSt, 18 minutes, color). Discusses the uses and potential benefits of testing infants and young children and demonstrates the use of the Gesell Infant Test.

Learning Disabilities (FHS, 19 minutes, color, VHS). Examines, through the case study of a nine-year-old boy, this frequently misdiagnosed and misunderstood condition. The importance of early diagnosis and treatment is emphasized.

Performance Assessment (1993, AIT, 45 minutes, color, VHS). The argument is advanced that standardized tests provide inadequate assessment of valuable educational goals such as cooperation, problem solving, and creativity. The case is made for the need for alternative strategies.

Preschoolers' Physical and Cognitive Development (1993, MS, 27 minutes, color, VHS). Illustrates the major areas to be assessed in the preschool child. Includes discussion of gross and fine motor skills, perceptual development, ways of learning, characteristics of thinking, and new uses of language.

Selecting an Achievement Test (1961, PSt, 14 minutes, b&w). Describes a method for analyzing achievement tests and common pitfalls in the selection process. Although dated, principles illustrated remain current.

Specific Learning Disabilities: Evaluation (1975, PSt, 27 minutes, color). Demonstrates the psycho-educational evaluation of two students with learning disabilities. Although film is dated, psycho-educational evaluation principles demonstrated remain current.

Standardized Tests: An Educational Tool (1961, PSt, 25 mins, color). Although dated, the film continues to illustrate issues related to selection of appropriate achievement tests. Concepts of reliability, validity, norms, distributions, and test interpretation are discussed in the context of an eighth-grade teacher selecting an appropriate group test to measure the reading abilities of her students.

Ways of Assessing Reading Progress (1975, PSt, 29 minutes, color). Although dated, film continues to illustrate strengths and limitations of reading tests. Reading experts discuss whether reading tests provide the educator with the information necessary to benefit students, parents, and teachers. Provides a more critical view of reading tests.

The Woodcock-Johnson Revised (1990, RivP, 1 hour, VHS). This videotape is of a teleconference of various experts discussing the W-J Revised and how it differs from the original version.

Who Is Pete? (1961, KU, 28 minutes, color/b&w). Although dated, this film continues to illustrate how the use of test results from a school's testing program can determine a particular student's strengths and weaknesses. Provides an overview of the variety of tests available in a school setting.

PART 4
PERSONALITY ASSESSMENT

CHAPTER 11
Personality Assessment: Overview and Objective Methods

Defining and Measuring "Personality"
    Traits, Types, and States
        Personality traits
        Personality types
        Personality states
    Measuring Personality
        Methods of personality assessment

Logical or Content Test Construction
    The Mooney Problem Checklist

Factor-Analytic Test Construction
    The 16 PF
    The NEO-PI and the NEO-PI-R

Test Construction by Empirical Criterion Keying
    The MMPI
    The MMPI-2
        The standardization sample
        Psychometric properties
        An evaluation
    The MMPI-A

The Theoretical Approach to Test Construction
    The Edwards Personal Preference Schedule (EPPS)

Clinical Versus Actuarial Predication

CLOSE-UP
    Limitations of Self-Report

EVERYDAY PSYCHOMETRICS
    Are Unisex Norms for the MMPI-2 Needed? Would They Work?

CLASS DISCUSSION QUESTIONS

Like *intelligence*, the word *personality* can and has been defined in a myriad of ways; a professor can probably cull as many different definitions of this word as there are students in the class. And so as we prepare to delve into the topic of personality assessment, some time devoted to enhancing the student's understanding of the subject matter to be assessed—personality—would appear to be in order. Here are some sample questions that may be asked at the beginning of class: How do you define personality? Which famous person is an example of someone with a "good" personality? Who has a "bad" personality? Who has no personality? Now go through this same list of questions with respect to famous children. Are the personality factors cited the same or different?

Another jumping-off point for discussion of this chapter relates to the question posed by the authors under the section Methods of Personality Assessment. Ask the class to think about how they might go about developing and validating a paper-and-pencil test of personality. What questions would they need to answer first?

Other potential class discussion questions are as follows:

1. Why measure personality?

2. The authors present their definition of personality in the chapter. A useful preliminary exercise and subsequent discussion prior to the assignment of reading Chapter 11 would ask students to write and then discuss their own definitions of personality. How do the various definitions presented in class compare with the more formal definitions/conceptions of personality presented in the chapter?

3. Compare and contrast with specific examples the terms *personality traits*, *states*, and *types*. Which term do you believe is most useful for behavioral description? Discuss the relevance of the concept of *situation-dependency* with respect to these terms.

4. Discuss why personality assessment is or is not necessary and/or important. In what settings and for what purposes is personality assessment useful?

5. If you were a test author, why might you want low test-retest reliability for a test that measures a state and high test-retest reliability for a test that measures a trait?

6. What are the advantages and limitations of the various methods of constructing personality tests by (a) logical or content test construction, (b) factor-analytic methods, (c) empirical criterion keying approach, and (d) theoretical approach?

7. If you were being considered for a job as a personnel psychologist, would you hope that your prospective employer was clinical or actuarial in his/her approach to evaluation? What about if you were undergoing counseling in the university counseling center; which approach would you hope the staff practiced?

8. As a follow-up to the chapter Close-Up, Limitations of Self-Report, summarize their limitations. How might these limitations be minimized, or is it not possible to address these limitations?

9. What are the problems inherent in rating scales for use in personality assessment?

10. Give examples from your own experience that relate to efforts of impression management in your own life (e.g., job interviews, first dates). How does this concept relate to personality assessment?

11. Give examples of your experience with rating scales. What impact might the halo effect, leniency or generosity, severity, or errors of central tendency have had on your ratings?

12. How do self-report personality inventories such as the MMPI-2 and the EPPS attempt to reduce the possibility of "faking"?

13. Consider the following statement (which is included in the narrative scoring report of the 16 PF): "Should be viewed as hypotheses to be validated against other sources of data." What does this statement mean? Review the factor analytic research on the 16 PF. What can you conclude?

14. Compare and contrast the criteria used in determining what makes a good personality test and those used in determining what makes a good intelligence or achievement test.

15. Compare and contrast not only the MMPI and the MMPI-2 but also the MMPI-2 and the MMPI-A. What characteristics of the MMPI contributed to the decision to revise it and extend it downward? What has contributed to its popularity as the world's most widely used and widely researched psychological test? What questions remain about the use of both tests for clinical practice? For research?

16. How are instruments used in personality testing that are "theory saturated" different from those that are relatively atheoretical? Provide some examples of each. Which would you prefer to use if you were a psychologist assessing the personality of your client?

17. Divide the class into two or more groups. As a follow-up to the chapter's Everyday Psychometrics section, have each group discuss the article presented in the section. Each group should respond to the following questions: Is there enough evidence to prohibit the use of the separate norms for each sex on the MMPI-2? If not, what additional research needs to be conducted?

CLASS DEMONSTRATIONS

1. Administer to the class a relatively brief, computer-scored personality inventory with all students taking it using a code name or number. Walk the students through the general approach to interpreting findings.

2. Invite a colleague specializing in clinical psychology to class to discuss the use of the MMPI-2 and/or 16 PF. The guest speaker could also be asked to share how other methods of objective assessment are used in clinical settings. Follow-up discussion can focus on the advantages and limitations for the use of these personality assessment approaches in clinical practice.

3. Invite a colleague to class to discuss the use of personality assessment approaches in research. Ask the guest speaker to bring in copies of instruments used in his/her work.

SUGGESTED ASSIGNMENTS

1. Using the questions to the reader relating to the development of an objective test of personality, have the students construct their own personality test. Students should address how they will avoid some of the limitations of self-report measures discussed in the chapter such as response styles and impression management. One example is an objective measure of anal character described in Davidson (1987) in which students working in groups constructed, administered, and evaluated their items for internal reliability and for convergent and discriminant validity. A more detailed manual for students in how to construct personality tests and to test hypotheses is provided in Geis (1978).

2. Each student chooses one of the personality tests discussed in Chapter 11. They then write summaries of current reviews of the chosen test using reference works such as the *Mental Measurements Yearbook, Test Critiques,* and journals such as the *Journal of Personality Assessment* or *Psychological Assessment: A Journal of Consulting and Clinical Psychology.*

3. Based on their reading, students are asked to prepare a one-page-or-less description of their own personal theory of personality. It can be an integration of all the theories presented in the chapter or one in particular. Suggestions regarding measurement in the context of this theory should also be included.

4. Assign students to research any of the numerous journal articles relating to the reliability and validity of the MMPI or MMPI-2. Ask them to prepare a written report and/or oral summary of the study they chose. The types of studies reviewed and trends in the reported findings could be discussed. Specifically, what types of reliability and validity evidence are presented in the article?

MEDIA RESOURCES

Dr. Gordon Allport, Part II (1967, AIM, 50 minutes, b&w). Dr. Allport discusses his theory of personality development.

Dr. Raymond Cattell, Parts I and II (1964, AIM, 50 minutes each part, b&w). Dr. Cattell discusses personality testing as well as issues related to intelligence, psychological testing, and psychotherapy.

Dr. Henry Murray, Part I (1963, AIM, 50 minutes, b&w). The esteemed personality theorist and developer of the TAT, Dr. Murray discusses his theory of personality.

Evaluating Personality (InsM, 45 minutes, color, VHS). Investigates various personality evaluation methods including the Rorschach, TAT, and MMPI. Traces historical development of assessment approaches by referring to astrology and phrenology. Intelligence and aptitude testing are also discussed.

Evaluating Personality: From Inkblots to Intuition (HRM, 45 minutes, color, VHS). Provides an overview of different types of personality evaluation, including astrology, phrenology, IQ testing, with specific guidance for conducting fair assessments.

Matching Job Types with Personality Types (RMI, 30 minutes, color, VHS). Discusses how to match unique personality types with the right career. Provides a practical illustration of the application of personality assessment to the "real world."

Personality (1971, IU, 30 minutes, color). Presents a brief discussion of various personality theories and the future of personality testing.

REFERENCES

Davidson, W. B. (1987). Undergraduate lab project in personality assessment: Measurement of anal character. *Teaching of Psychology, 14,* 101–103.

Geis, F. (1978). *Personality research manual.* New York: Wiley.

Hall, C. S., & Lindzey, G. (1978). *Theories of personality.* (3d Ed). New York: Wiley.

CHAPTER 12
Projective Methods

CLASS DISCUSSION QUESTIONS

As a means of an entree into a discussion of the theory and practice of projective testing, you may wish to actually attempt the exercise described at the beginning of this chapter:

> Suppose the lights in your classroom were dimmed and everyone was told to stare at the clean chalkboard for about a minute or so. And suppose everyone was then asked to take out some paper and write down what they thought they could "see" on the chalkboard—other than the chalkboard itself.

> Assuming none of your students are extremely oppositional or actively hallucinating (or both), this type of exercise may be quite instructive. One word of caution if you do chance it: Make sure the chalkboard or portion of it you ask the students to focus on is not only clean but free of visible scratch marks; otherwise, students may in essence be associating to line drawings.

Other potential class discussion questions are as follows:

1. Compare projective techniques to other methods of personality assessment covered to this point. What are the features of each? What are the advantages and limitations of each?

2. Discuss the different types of stimuli that are used to create projective tests (words, pictures, inkblots, etc.). What type(s) of stimuli might contribute to more valid tests?

3. How might you go about exploring the technical adequacy (i.e., reliability and validity) of a test such as the Rorschach?

4. How does the validity evidence provided for tests such as the TAT, the Rorschach, and figure-drawing tests stack up with respect to the standards presented in the *Standards for Educational and Psychological Testing* (1985)?

5. Is it possible to "fake good" on the Rorschach? On the TAT? On sentence completion tests?

6. What do you think accounts for the popularity of projective methods (in spite of a lack of psychometric soundness)?

7. What are the assumptions on which projective methods are based? Are these assumptions supported by the research to date?

8. How might figure drawings be particularly valuable in the personality assessment of young children or illiterates?

CLASS DEMONSTRATIONS

1. Select a series of pictures from a magazine (e.g., *Life*) and have them duplicated for the class. In addition (or alternatively), the one printed in the chapter (A TAT-like Picture) can be used. This will represent a simulation of the TAT. Students are asked to administer the set of pictures to at least three subjects and record their responses verbatim. During class time, discussion can focus on the advantages and disadvantages of this method for personality assessment and actually developing a scoring system.

2. The goals of the following exercise include: (1) to demonstrate how the Rorschach is administered; (2) to involve students in reacting to ambiguous stimuli; (3) to allow students to experience obtaining test results; and (4) to challenge students' implicit methods of evaluating tests. The exercise will take approximately 45 minutes, but must span two class periods.

Step 1: Administration Demonstration

The instructor develops four inkblots by spreading ink in the center of a white sheet of paper and folding the paper in half. The same blots are used each year, which allows the instructor to establish a set of common responses ("populars") to the blots. The blots are numbered so that they are presented in a particular order, and they are marked as to which side is "up" when presented to the subject.

By way of explanation of how the test is administered, the instructor demonstrates the administration to the class. The instructor notes that the actual Rorschach inkblots are not used and the class is asked to give a rationale for that decision (i.e., test security; refer to *Standards*).

A volunteer from the class is solicited and the class is informed that the volunteer will have the identical experience as someone in a typical Exner-type Rorschach session except for the presence and involvement of the audience.

Students in the audience are asked to take out a blank sheet of paper, and write a code name on the top. The audience will record their own responses on this paper. The instructor collects all of the papers at the end of the class and they are returned by the code name to assure anonymity. As in the typical Rorschach administration, the examiner (instructor) records the responses of the volunteer.

The volunteer is invited up and the instructor sits at a right angle to him/her. The instructor points out this seating arrangement to the class. The instructor assumes the role of the examiner by reciting the following instructions:

> The test I'm going to give you today is called the Rorschach. Have you ever heard of it or taken it? In this test, I will show you a series of inkblots and will want you to tell me what you see. Do you understand? (Does the audience understand?)

The first card is shown to the audience first and then the query, "What might this be?" Give the class time to respond.

The card is then shown to the volunteer subject: "What might this be?" (Record response and remember to say, "Most people see more than one thing in each card" if the first card elicits only one response.)

Administer all four cards, then go back for Exner-style inquiry: "I want to be able to see it like you do." (Record inquiry.)

The responses are then collected from the class.

The demonstration typically is followed by a lengthy discussion about administration, of the what-happens-if type: What if the subject turns the card? What if the subject has no response? Students often note the copious notes the instructor takes during the administration and wonder why. Ask the students about whether there are any skeptics relating to the validity of the test (i.e., that the test does not tell us something valuable about the person).

Step 2: Test Results

Before the next class period, the instructor attaches to each page of responses received from audience members (and also the volunteer's responses) a "Feedback Sheet" containing an interpretation (see below). The interpretation is attached to the back of the response sheet so that students do not see each other's interpretations.

At the next class, the students pass the pile of responses and interpretations around, picking up their own. They are asked to read the interpretation sheet and respond to the questions on the bottom. Prior to initiating the discussion, the instructor polls the students as to their responses to the first question, and typically finds that the students feel the interpretation is quite accurate.

A discussion follows, prompted by the instructor inquiring as to people's reactions. At some point in the discussion, it becomes evident that everyone received the same feedback; and the students get a good laugh. The class then addresses this issue: Why did the feedback seem accurate when it was the same for everyone?

Often students have a sense of this in that they note the test interpretations sound like a horoscope. This provides an opportunity to introduce the Barnum effect. The instructor emphasizes that, in deciding about the validity of a test, students should not depend on their subjective opinions about whether or not the test "worked" for them.

Given this discussion, the instructor poses the question: How can test developers and researchers accurately evaluate the validity of a projective test like the Rorschach? This also provides a springboard to a discussion of the specific psychometric characteristics of the Rorschach.

Inkblot Response Profile

PLEASE READ YOUR PROFILE RESULTS PRIVATELY AND ANSWER THE QUESTIONS BELOW.

This profile has been scored on four factors: A through D. You have a numerical score on each factor, as indicated below. A brief description follows each factor score.

Response profile: #12

Response pattern: 1-5-9-2

Factor A. Score = 1. INTERPRETATION: The degree to which the subject is willing/able to experience a satisfying connection with others varies with the social situation. Sometimes the subject is willing to share himself/herself with others; at other times, the subject prefers to maintain emotional distance.

Factor B. Score = 5. INTERPRETATION: The subject may be experiencing some intrapsychic stress, but appears to have sufficient intrapersonal resources to cope with the stress.

Factor C. Score = 9. INTERPRETATION: The subject's self-image fluctuates. Sometimes the subject experiences himself/herself as competent and skilled, but at other times the self-perception is more negative, focusing on experienced deficits in skills and cognition. Most of these experienced deficits are not objectively present in the subject, as the subject is quite intelligent.

Factor D. Score = 2. INTERPRETATION: The subject tolerates authority. Because the subject considers himself/herself to be a free thinker, the subject notices deficiencies in authority figures and may become frustrated at not feeling able to voice these observations.

To the subject: Please answer the following questions:

To what degree does the above profile fit you own perceptions of yourself?

Please circle your response.

    a very poor fit   1 2 3 4 5 6 7   a perfect fit

Did the profile printed above reveal anything about your personality of which you had not been aware?

    nothing   maybe one or two things   several things

3. As a class project, make up a word association and/or sentence completion test (see the relevant sections of Chapter 12 for a start). Administer it to at least three subjects. As a class, discuss the results and possible methods of scoring.

4. A trained clinical psychologist with experience with the Rorschach can be invited to class as a guest speaker. The guest speaker could discuss his or her varied experiences with the method, situations in which it has been most useful, guidelines related to how and when it should be used, and issues related to the administration and interpretation of the test. The guest speaker can also share other types of projective tests such as sentence-completion tests and picture-story tests that are used in clinical settings.

5. A school psychologist can be invited to class to discuss the use of projective tests in the school setting. Follow-up discussion might include how the use of projective tests differ in the school versus clinical settings. One interesting format might include a panel of school, clinical, industrial, and counseling psychologists discussing how projective tests are used in various settings in which they work and what characteristics of those settings contribute to their differential uses. Also ask guest speakers to address the psychometric characteristics of the tests and how this influences the tests' use in each setting.

6. Two faculty colleagues could be invited to class—one who favors the use of projective methods and one who will debate against their use. Students are asked to take notes on their debate and prepare a written summary of both speakers' opinions. A concluding statement as to who "won" the debate should also be included.

7. During a group administration, the instructor administers the Draw-A-Person: Screening Procedure for Emotional Disturbance, as discussed in the chapter Close-Up and in the section on Machover's Draw-A-Person Test. After administration and discussion of some of the more salient characteristics used in interpretation of the drawings as described in the text, discuss the students' reactions to the reliability and validity evidence presented in the chapter Close-Up. Would they recommend the use of this approach in schools? In clinical practice with adults?

SUGGESTED ASSIGNMENTS

1. Have students score the TAT-like stories in the chapter using the scoring criteria discussed.

2. Each student chooses one of the projective methods discussed in Chapter 12. Students are asked to locate and summarize in writing current reviews of their test in reference books such as the *Mental Measurements Yearbook* and/or *Test Critiques*, and/or relevant journals such as the *Journal of Personality Assessment*.

3. As a follow-up to the Everyday Psychometrics section, divide the class into two groups to form a panel debate on the pros and cons of projective methods of personality assessment. Assign one group the position of being in favor of their use; the other is in opposition to using projective techniques. In order to obtain information to support their position, students are assigned the responsibility of researching the relevant journals related to personality assessment. They can also consult with practicing clinicians in the community or on the faculty (including the winner and loser described in class demonstration #6).

MEDIA RESOURCES

Administration of Projective Tests (1951, PSt, 10 minutes, b&w). Demonstrates administration of common projective tests such as the TAT, sentence-completion, word-association, Szondi, and draw-a-person tests. Although film is dated, demonstrations of all but the Szondi test remain relevant.

Dr. Henry Murray, Part I (50 minutes, AIM, b&w). Dr. Murray discusses the TAT and Rorschach Projective methods.

Personality (1971, IU, 30 minutes, color). Illustrates the use and presents a critical review of the Draw-A-Person, Holtzman Inkblot, and the TAT projective methods of personality assessment.

CHAPTER 13
Other Personality and Behavioral Measures

Self-Report/Self-Rating Methods
    Self-Concept Measures
        The Beck Self-Concept Test
        Piers-Harris Children's Self-Concept Scale
        Q-sort techniques
        Adjective checklists
        Self-concept differentiation
    Locus of Control
    Learning Styles

Situational Performance Measures
    The Character Education Inquiry
    Leaderless-Group Situations
    Situational Stress Tests

Measures of Cognitive Style
    Field Dependence and Independence
        The Group Embedded Figures Test
    Reflective Versus Impulsive Cognitive Styles
    Leveling Versus Sharpening

Behavioral Assessment
    An Overview
    The Who, What, When, Where, and How of It
    Behavioral Observation and Behavior Rating Scales
        The Social Skills Rating System
        The Self-Injury Trauma (SIT) Scale
    Analogue Studies
    Self-Monitoring
    Role-Play
    Unobtrusive Measures
    Issues in Behavioral Assessment

Psychophysiological Assessment
    Biofeedback
    The Polygraph
    Plethysmography
    Pupillary Responses

Ratings of Personality and Behavior by Others
    The Personality Inventory for Children
    Potential Limitations of Rating Scales
        The rater
        The instrument
        The context of evaluation

CLOSE-UP
    Confessions of a Behavior Rater

EVERYDAY PSYCHOMETRICS
    Classical Versus Generalizability Theory in Psychometric Evaluation

CLASS DISCUSSION QUESTIONS

In this chapter situational performance measures including situational stress tests (such as the type of test that might be required for employment as a stockbroker) are discussed. What other types of situational stress tests can students envision? How might a situational stress test be designed to screen psychologists for a position as an instructor of a course in tests and measurements? These and related questions may be used as a stimulus to thought and discussion of some of the issues in this chapter.

Other potential class discussion questions are as follows:

1. Has anyone in the class had experience with any of the tools in personality assessment discussed in Chapter 13? What about a polygraph? Based on the material presented in the text, do students agree or disagree with the decision not to allow the results of polygraph tests to be introduced as evidence in court? Why or why not?

2. Why might a psychologist be interested in an individual's self-concept? A tendency for being field dependent/independent? Being impulsive or reflective? Whether their locus of control is internal or external? Whether they are a leveler or sharpener? In what settings and for what purposes might a professional be interested in measuring these constructs?

3. Discussion can occur regarding the major differences between behavioral and traditional assessment. The table included in the chapter can serve as a useful jumping-off point. The instructor can provide examples of the use of various behavioral and traditional assessment techniques.

4. Discuss the limitations of behavioral observation. How might these limitations be minimized? Identify problems other than those listed in the text associated with behavioral observation as an assessment technique.

5. Compare and contrast the "sign" approach to assessment versus the "sample" approach. What are the features of each? Give examples of each. Discuss their relationship to the traditional and behavioral views of personality.

6. Compare and contrast the different types of behavioral assessment including behavior rating scales and psychophysiological methods. How are rating scales categorized?

7. Define self-concept and discuss the various methods of assessing this construct.

8. Discuss possible uses for a measure such as the Social Skills Rating Scale (SSRS).

9. Discuss the various uses of role-play in assessment as compared to teaching and therapy. Provide examples.

10. How might the reliability and validity of behavioral observation methods be determined? How do these methods compare with other types of personality assessment? Projective tests? Objective personality tests?

11. What factors affect the reliability and validity of behavioral measures (such as definition of the target behavior, contrast effect, reactivity)?

12. How generalizable are the findings from the behavioral methods? Prior to raising this question, be certain students recognize the significance of the concept of generalizability.

13. Discuss the advantage of generalizability theory as opposed to classical test theory in determining the reliability of behavioral measures. Refer the students back to the chapter's Everyday Psychometrics section on Classical versus Generalizability Theory in Psychometric Evaluation.

14. Discuss the various "tools" of behavioral assessment.

15. Discuss the problems inherent in rating scales for use in personality assessment.

16. Give examples of your experience with rating scales. What impact might the halo effect, leniency or generosity, severity, or errors of central tendency have had on your ratings? How do response styles relate to personality assessment? Give an example of each. How does feedback or the lack of it to the testtaker relate to personality assessment?

CLASS DEMONSTRATIONS

1. Invite to class a trained polygraph administrator who would be asked to discuss his or her opinions and experiences with a polygraph, discuss particular cases/situations in which it has been useful, discuss guidelines for appropriate use, and give suggestions for administration and interpretation. A polygraph expert might be located from within the judicial system, the local police department, a field office of the FBI, or a private security firm.

2. Obtain one or more of the tests discussed in Chapter 13 such as the Matching Familiar Figures Test (Kagan, 1966) and administer it to the class for the purposes of illustration and discussion.

3. Invite to class a guest speaker on the use of biofeedback in personality assessment and therapy. A faculty member with a joint appointment in the student counseling center or who is also in independent practice might be a good resource in this area.

4. A clinical or counseling psychologist, specializing in behavior therapy, can be invited to class to provide examples of behavioral principles and techniques used in his or her practice. The instructor and students can then relate the information presented to material contained in the text.

5. Invite as a guest speaker a faculty colleague or an industrial/organizational psychologist who works in the community to speak on the use of situational performance measures and situational stress tests in business and industry.

6. Divide students into groups and ask them to develop situational performance measures for various types of jobs (e.g., college professor, cook). If possible, the class can actually implement in a role-playing situation one or more performance measures that were developed and judged to be the best by the class. Discussion can then turn to what the observers would focus on during the role-play and how to assess the reliability and validity of this assessment approach.

7. Divide students into two groups for a debate on traditional versus behavioral assessment. Students can utilize information presented in the chapter, refer to content they have been exposed to in other classes, and review some of the relevant literature in professional journals.

8. Bring to class examples of some of the common behavior rating scales used with children and adolescents such as the Child Behavior Checklist, Revised Behavior Problem Checklist, or the Behavior Rating Scale and the Personality Inventory for Children. Then discuss the strengths and limitations of indirect measures of behavior.

9. Administer a commonly used measure of self-concept to the class. Subsequent discussion can focus on the limitations of such data.

SUGGESTED ASSIGNMENTS

1. Each student chooses one of the tools in personality assessment discussed in Chapter 13. Students then locate and summarize in writing current reviews of their test from reference books such as the *Mental Measurements Yearbook* and/or *Test Critiques*.

2. Have the students contact local businesses and industry and interview the personnel director about their use of various methods of personality assessment (e.g., polygraph, situational performance measures) in hiring and promotion practices.

3. Students are assigned various problem situations and asked to develop unobtrusive observation measures for learning more about them. Include, for example, problems such as not completing homework, doing poorly in math class, and lack of assertiveness.

4. Divide students into groups and ask them to create their own social skills rating form. Students can draw from information on these forms presented in the chapter.

5. Drawing upon information presented in the section The Who, What, Where, and How of It, divide students in two or more groups. Give each group a target behavior (e.g., the number of times students get up for a study break in the library), and ask them to develop their own behavioral observation tool, conduct the observations, and report reliability data. Discuss their reactions to serving as a "rater" and relate to the information presented in the chapter Close-Up on Confessions of a Behavior Rater.

MEDIA RESOURCES

Assessment and Prevention of Aggressive Behaviors in Patients (1993, FAV, 30 minutes, color, VHS). Defines aggressive behavior and describes factors that increase its risk. Behavioral indicators used to assess a client's potential for aggressive behavior are identified and interventions are discussed.

Behavioral Assessment for School Psychologists (1983, NASP, 50 minutes, color, VHS). Videotape includes demonstrations of various methods of behavioral observation referred to in Chapter 13 (e.g., duration recording). Issues related to subject reactivity, unobtrusive measures, and assessing the reliability of the observations are addressed.

Behavior Modification: Teaching Language to Psychotic Children (1969, PSt, 42 minutes, color). Demonstrates a number of behavioral assessment techniques discussed in the chapter. Features work of Ivar Lovass in teaching autistic children speech for spontaneous conversation.

Behavioral Therapy Demonstration (1969, PSt, 32 minutes, color). Demonstrates behavioral methods of therapy including assessment of the client's anxiety. Illustrates concepts presented in the chapter related to behavior therapy and assessment.

Conscience of a Child (1963, PSt, 30 minutes, b&w). Demonstrates some of the methods used in the laboratory of Dr. R. Sears to study conscience development in children. In particular, methods such as those described in the section on situational performance measures are depicted.

Experimental Studies in Social Climates of Groups (1953, PSt, 32 minutes, b&w). Depicts variation of use of a situational performance measure (leaderless group situation) to study the behavior of children under autocratic, democratic, and laissez-faire group conditions (Lewin, Lippitt, and White studies with the use of a hidden camera).

Frustration Play Techniques (1942, PSt, 35 minutes, b&w). Demonstrates use of play procedures to assess personality, a situation performance measure referred to in Chapter 13.

Observation (1993, MS, 27 minutes, color, VHS). Discusses various reasons for observing children and observation techniques including types and components of naturalistic and subjective approaches. Difficulties in observing and recording are also addressed.

Dr. Carl Rogers, Part I (1969, PSt, 50 minutes, color). Dr. Rogers discusses his theory of personality and development of client-centered therapy. Can supplement the material in the chapter dealing with measures of self-concept.

REFERENCE

Kagan, J. (1966). Reflection-impulsivity: The generality and dynamics of conceptual tempo. *Journal of Abnormal Psychology, 71,* 17–24.

PART 5
TESTING AND ASSESSMENT IN ACTION

CHAPTER 14
Clinical and Counseling Assessment

An Overview

The Interview
    The Mental Status Examination
    Other Specialized Interviews

The Case History

Psychological Tests
    The Psychological Test Battery
    Diagnostic Tests
        The Millon tests
    Measures of Depression
        Beck Depression Inventory
        Children's Depression Inventory
        Other measures of depression
    Measures of Values
        The Study of Values
        The Rokeach Values Survey
        The Work Values Inventory
    Other Tests

Special Applications of Clinical Measures
    Forensic Psychological Assessment
        Competency to stand trial
        Criminal responsibility
        Readiness for parole or probation
    Custody Evaluations
        Evaluation of the parent
        Evaluation of the child
    Child Abuse and Neglect
        Physical signs of abuse and neglect
        Emotional and behavioral signs of abuse and neglect
        Risk assessment
    Assessment in Health Psychology

The Psychological Report
    Writing the Clinical Report
    The Barnum Effect

CLOSE-UP
    Marital and Family Assessment

EVERYDAY PSYCHOMETRICS
    Psychometric Aspects of the Interview

CLASS DISCUSSION QUESTIONS

Table 13–1, in the previous chapter, summarizes some of the distinctions between behavioral assessment and more traditional approaches to assessment. Following a presentation and a discussion of these distinctions, it may be useful to have students continue their debate of the merits of each of these approaches to assessment in a *clinical* context. Examples of the use of these two approaches in the clinical settings should also be emphasized.

Other potential class discussion questions are as follows:

1. Have you had any recent experiences with being interviewed (e.g., employment interview)? Was the interviewer warm and accepting or cool and aloof? Were open- or closed-ended questions posed? Did you feel the interviewer understood you? How did the interviewer attempt to put you at ease? Was it structured or unstructured? Based on your reading of the chapter's Everyday Psychometrics section, Psychometric Aspects of the Interview, how might the reliability and validity of the type interview in which you were a participant be assessed?

2. Compare and contrast clinical and counseling psychologists in relation to their use of psychological tests.

3. Why is face validity a problem with the Beck Depression Inventory?

4. What do the Barnum and Aunt Fanny effects tell a psychologist about what to include and what *not* to include when writing a psychological report?

5. Discuss the various measures of depression presented in the text. Differentiate diagnostic from screening measures. Which appears to be the most reliable and valid based on the information presented?

6. What is forensic psychological assessment? In what specific contexts might it be used (e.g., competency to stand trial, criminal responsibility, child-custody evaluations, readiness for parole or probation, signs of child abuse and neglect)?

7. Identify the emotional and behavioral indications of child abuse and neglect. How are these assessed by the psychologist? Discuss the reasoning of why tests that measure risk of child abuse are not permissible in court. How is the concept of base rate related to this decision?

8. Encourage students to respond to the question posed at the end of the chapter Close-Up: From what you know of the Bundys—or some other family, even your own—what types of responses would you expect to find on the marital and family assessment? How might such data be used therapeutically to make each family member's life, as well as the family as a whole, more fulfilling?

CLASS DEMONSTRATIONS

1. A guest speaker for the day could be a practicing clinical or counseling psychologist who is a skilled interviewer. The clinician could discuss the importance of interviews, how to make them maximally effective, and particularly difficult interviews to conduct. It would also be helpful if the guest speaker could role-play with a volunteer from the class an actual interview. Such a guest speaker could also address the issue of the use of the DSM-IV for diagnostic purposes and the diagnosis of depression.

2. Bring to class a structured interview such as the Structured Clinical Interview, the Structured Pediatric Interview, or the Child Assessment Schedule, and have one student administer to another (role-play) student.

3. One or more guest speakers could be invited to class to discuss the issue of the use of psychological assessment for forensic purposes. It would be most interesting if the instructor could invite one or more psychologists who specialize in forensic psychology and representatives from the judicial

system, including a lawyer and a judge. The speakers could discuss the issues and concerns related to assessments for competency to stand trial, criminal responsibility, readiness for parole or probation, and child custody evaluations.

4. A volunteer class member playing the role of a person in a DSM-IV diagnostic category could be administered a mental status exam by the instructor or a colleague trained in its use. Based on this demonstration, discuss the advantages and limitations of this assessment tool.

5. Divide the class into two groups. Assign one group the position of defending the use of mental health professionals as expert witnesses. Assign the other group the con position. Encourage students to review the references cited in the chapter as well as additional sources to prepare for the "debate."

6. Invite to class a specialist from the state or county child protection agency or perhaps a colleague who specializes in this area to speak about the role of psychological assessment in the determination of child abuse and neglect. Do they conduct risk assessments? If so, what does it consist of?

7. Invite to class a marriage and family therapist. Have the therapist read the chapter Close-Up prior to their talk, and request that he or she comment on their own assessment of a couple and/or family and how it compares or contrasts with what is presented in the Close-Up.

8. In the section Measures of Values, the reader is asked to rank-order the lists of values presented. Using Rokeach (1973), discuss the meaning of the results for individual students.

9. The instructor can bring in various examples of psychological reports (these can be obtained from books on psychological report writing found in many university libraries). Try to find reports that include measurement terms studied earlier in the course such as standard error of measurement, confidence interval, standard score, mean, standard deviation, and so on. Students can form groups with each one having the task of reviewing a different report and critiquing it for readability.

10. Invite to class a colleague or psychologist in the community who specializes in child custody evaluations. Ask the guest speaker to describe the psychological assessment approaches used as part of that evaluation. Has consideration been given to the reliability and validity of the assessment approaches/instruments used?

SUGGESTED ASSIGNMENTS

1. Each student chooses one of the assessment methods (such as structured interviews, Millon tests, or assessment instruments used in forensic work) discussed in Chapter 14. Students then locate and summarize in writing current reviews of their test in reference books such as the *Mental Measurements Yearbook*. They can also include a section that addresses the uses of the method for counseling and/or clinical purposes. Are the conclusions reached by the students consistent with those presented by the authors?

2. Students can be given the assignment to review local papers or national media for examples of court cases in which the determination of a defendant's sanity or insanity and/or psychological testimony was a prominent part of the trial. Discussion can follow relating to role of forensic psychological assessment.

MEDIA RESOURCES

Assessment and Diagnosis of Childhood Psychopathology (1980, PSt, 26 minutes, color). Familiarizes the student with the DSM-II and DSM-III classification systems. The film also illustrates the psychiatric assessment and diagnosis with children including an interview and diagnostic play session with a child with Down's syndrome.

Descending to Danger (1988, ITS, 17 minutes, color, VHS). Depicts methods to identify and evaluate the seriousness of depression.

Highlights of the DSM-IV (1994, APA, 180 minutes, color, VHS). Provides a brief overview of the DSM-IV with particular attention to how it differs from its previous edition, DSM-III R.

The Interview Film: What to Know and What to Do (1977, IU, 21 minutes, color). Demonstrates and analyzes the interviewing procedure from the employer's point of view. Includes five interviews with candidates for a position of cashier in a restaurant chain. A supplementary class exercise could include the students rating each interview on the dimensions discussed in the chapter.

Introduction to Behavioral Counseling (1975, PSt, 26 minutes, color). Demonstrates through the use of a case study how a behavioral counselor works with a client. Illustrates the principles presented in the chapter relating to behavioral assessment and theory.

Psychoanalysis (1964, PSt, 30 minutes, color). Enactment of several sessions of analytic sessions. Illustrates several clinical/counseling interviewing techniques discussed in the chapter.

Psychological Response (1975, PSt, 13 minutes, b&w). Illustrates the various clinical/counseling interviewing techniques discussed in the chapter. A counselor helps three people assess their feelings and deal with the guilt that resulted from living through a natural disaster.

REFERENCE

Rokeach, M. (1973). *The nature of human values.* New York: The Free Press.

CHAPTER 15

Neuropsychological Assessment

The Nervous System and Behavior
    Neurological Damage and the Concept of "Organicity"

The Neuropsychological Examination
    The History
    The Neuropsychological Mental Status Examination
    The Physical Examination

Neuropsychological Tests
    Specialized Interviews and Rating Scales
    Intellectual Ability Tests in Neuropsychology
    Memory Tests
    Tests of Cognitive Functioning
    Tests of Verbal Functioning
    Perceptual, Motor, and Perceptual-Motor Tests
        The Bender-Visual Motor Gestalt Test

Neuropsychological Test Batteries
    The "Flexible" Battery
    The Prepackaged Battery
        Halstead-Reitan Neuropsychological Battery
        Luria-Nebraska Neuropsychological Battery
        Other neuropsychological batteries

A Perspective

CLOSE-UP
    Medical Diagnostic Aids in Neuropsychological Examinations

EVERYDAY PSYCHOMETRICS
    Validity of the LNNB

CLASS DISCUSSION QUESTIONS

Components of a neurological examination include (1) the history, (2) the neuropsychological mental status examination, (3) the physical examination, and (4) neurological testing. Ask students, from their own background and experience, to think of a neuropsychological disorder with which they have some familiarity (e.g., epilepsy, Alzheimer's, etc.) and then discuss how an individual suffering from such a disorder might present upon examination with respect to each of the assessment techniques listed above.

Other potential class discussion questions are as follows:

1. Discuss the differences and similarities between "brain damage," "neurological damage," and "organicity."

2. Discuss the evidence for the nonunitary nature of organicity.

3. How do the neurologist and neuropsychologist work together and complement each other? Differentiate their responsibilities.

4. Why is it essential for a neuropsychological evaluation to include a history taking, a mental status examination, and the administration of a neuropsychological test battery? Why is it a good practice for diagnostic decisions not to be based on the results of one measure?

5. Distinguish between organic and functional disorders. Why is this distinction important?

6. List and discuss some of the physical examination procedures that neuropsychologists can perform (noninvasive), and what area of functioning each measure is designed to tap.

7. What are the advantages and limitations of both "flexible batteries" and "prepackaged batteries" in neuropsychological assessment?

8. What are the common types of validity evidence presented for neuropsychological test batteries?

9. Why are memory, cognitive functioning, verbal functioning, perceptual, motor, and perceptual-motor tests included in a chapter on neuropsychological assessment?

10. As a follow-up to the chapter's Everyday Psychometrics section, Validity of the LNNB, discuss the issues related to the criterion-related, content, and construct validity of the test. What conclusions can be made about the test's validity?

11. Why is the Bender more popular among nonneuropsychologists than with neuropsychologists? Based on the psychometric data presented in the chapter, what conclusions can be made about the Bender as a neurological diagnostic instrument? What about its use for assessing personality?

12. As a follow-up to the chapter's Close-Up on Medical Diagnostic Aids in Neuropsychological Examinations, ask students to share any experiences they or any family members or friends have had with any of the procedures described in the Close-Up.

CLASS DEMONSTRATIONS

1. Invite to class as a guest speaker a neuropsychologist to describe job responsibilities as well as the types of assessment methods used. A neurologist may also be invited to speak. Both could address areas of collaboration. Your local hospital's physical rehabilitation section or your own department may be a good referral source to locate these speakers.

2. Bring to class actual neuropsychological tests discussed in Chapter 15 such as the Wechsler Memory Scale—Revised or Bender Gestalt. Parts of these tests could be administered to volunteer subjects. The Bender can be group administered.

3. Contact a colleague who teaches your department's physiological psychology class to serve as a guest speaker to supplement material on brain/behavior relationships that is presented in the chapter. Ask this speaker to utilize models of the human brain to supplement the presentation if possible.

SUGGESTED ASSIGNMENTS

1. Each student chooses one of the neuropsychological tests discussed in Chapter 15. The instructor should be sure that all types of tests are represented (e.g., memory, perceptual, etc.). Students are asked to locate and summarize in writing current reviews of their test in reference books such as the *Mental Measurements Yearbook*. These reports will form the content of oral presentations on the various test instruments.

2. Assign students to design a map of the brain with reference to various brain/behavior relationships. In addition, specify examples of neuropsychological assessment tests/subtests to assess functioning in these areas of the brain.

3. Assign students one or more specific sensory and motor deficits presented in Chapter 15 (e.g., acalcula, anopia, ataxia). Their task is to specify what areas of the brain are involved in the assigned deficit and how they would go about assessing it using one or more of the tests described in Chapter 15.

MEDIA RESOURCES

Brain and Behavior (1963, PSt, 30 minutes, b&w). Demonstrates various brain/behavior relationships and how electrical activity in the brain gives information about human behavior.

The Brain-Mind Connection (1990, InsM, 30 minutes, color). Neuroscientists explain the structure and function of the human brain. They discuss research findings related to the two hemispheres and implications of enriched versus impoverished environments on brain development. Profiles a young boy recovering from a hemispherectomy.

The Brain-Damaged Child (1968, PSt, 31 minutes, b&w). Illustrates some of the behavior patterns associated with organicity. Also demonstrates the use of stress during the interview as part of the neuropsychological assessment.

Correlates of Performance on Spatial Aptitude Tests (1979, InLP, 12 minutes, color). Demonstrates use of spatial tasks for neuropsychological screening. Includes demonstration of the EEG.

Development of the Human Brain (1990, PSt, 46 minutes, color, VHS). Follows the physical development of the brain from conception through the moment of birth to age eight.

Impairment of the Abstract Attitude as Shown on the Cube Test (1950, MiDW, 19 minutes, color). Demonstrates use of the Cube Test to assess nonverbal abstract reasoning.

Left Brain, Right Brain—Part 1: Left Brain (1979, PSt, 28 minutes, color). Describes lateral specialization of the brain with a focus on the left hemisphere.

Left Brain, Right Brain—Part II: Right Brain (1979, PSt, 24 minutes, color). Discusses the theorized functions of the right brain. Presents case studies and real-life examples demonstrating that the right brain is responsible for spatial perception.

Neurological Examination of the Newborn (1960, PSt, 30 minutes, color). Demonstrates a neurological examination and normal and abnormal responses of infants.

Neurological Examination of the One-Year-Old (1960, PSt, 30 minutes, color). Demonstrates a neurological examination and normal and abnormal responses of one-year-olds.

Perceptual-Motor Evaluation of a Child with Dysfunction (1967, CLU, 33 minutes, b&w). Demonstrates the use of standard and nonstandard tests in assessing the degree of perceptual-motor dysfunction in a seven-year-old with a neurological deficit.

Perceptual-Motor Evaluation of a Perceptually Normal Child (1967, CLU, 33 minutes, b&w). Demonstrates the use of standardized and nonstandardized tests as a method of assessing visual, tactile, and kinesthetic perception and related motor functions.

CHAPTER 16

The Assessment of People with Disabling Conditions

CLASS DISCUSSION QUESTIONS

Can a psychologist apply the norms of a test standardized on people without disabling conditions to a nonstandardized administration of the test to people with disabilities? Such a thought-provoking question may be useful in stimulating class discussion with regard to the issues attendant to the testing of people with disabling conditions.

Other potential class discussion questions are as follows:

1. What types of modification are necessary to conduct reliable and valid psychological assessments of children and adults with different types of disabling conditions (e.g., vision, hearing, deaf/blind, motor, cognitive)?

2. Why not use only intelligence tests in the assessment of mental retardation?

3. Why have hearing-impaired and deaf children often been mistakenly diagnosed as mentally retarded or emotionally disturbed in the past? Why is there a need for a complete evaluation including different tests, interviews, observations, history taking, and review of all relevant records? Information on the case study method from the chapters on clinical and counseling assessment can be integrated into this discussion.

4. Name three different standardized testing instruments. Now, discuss how each could be modified for individuals with motor disabilities. The problem of deviating from the standardized procedures and its implications for using the norms can be discussed again here. This discussion may start in a small-group situation, and then student representatives from each group could report to the whole class.

5. Identify the subtests of commonly used intelligence tests (e.g., Wechsler, Stanford-Binet Fourth Edition, and K-ABC) that can be administered to the hearing impaired.

6. Discuss the issue of personality assessment of the hearing impaired. What special challenges does this present for the examiner? What types of measures are typically used, and what are their advantages and limitations? Compare and contrast these challenges when assessing individuals with cognitive, visual, or motor disabilities.

7. Compare and contrast measures of adaptive behavior with the social skills rating scales presented in Chapter 13.

8. How does the examiner answer the question of the relevancy of the norms when comparing an examinee with a disability with nondisabled peers or with those who have disabling conditions?

9. As a follow-up to the chapter's Everyday Psychometrics section, Psychometric Evaluation of the Vineland, have the class respond to the question posed at the start of the section: What specific types of reliability and validity do they believe should be available for this test? Review the reliability and validity evidence presented in this section. Do they agree with the conclusions of the authors regarding the psychometric adequacy of this instrument?

10. Discuss the issue of how much validity data is necessary to meet the section of the federal law cited early in the chapter relating to the legal requirement that psychologists assessing individuals with disabling conditions only "use tests and other assessment materials which have been validated for the specific purpose for which they are being used." Review the various federal laws related to the disabled including which types of disabilities are covered under each.

CLASS DEMONSTRATIONS

1. The instructor or a student can administer parts of a standardized achievement test to a volunteer from the class who simulates a particular type of exceptionality. For example, the student can wear a blindfold to simulate a visual handicap. Students can also be asked to use their nondominant hand in completing written items or take a test with their arms tied behind their back to simulate motor impairments (see Carroll [1974] and McCallum [1979] for additional ideas for simulating various types of disabilities). Subsequent class discussion can focus on the types of modifications in testing procedures that would be necessary to ensure a valid and reliable assessment.

2. The school psychologist from the local school district or psychologist from a local hospital clinic can be invited as a guest speaker to discuss the assessment of exceptional children. The talk might focus on the types of adaptations often necessary for completing a reliable and valid psychological assessment as well as the types of tests developed specifically for a particular type of disability. Legal requirements relating to assessment of individuals with disabilities should also be covered.

3. The instructor can bring to class actual psychological reports (with all personally identifiable information deleted) for individuals suspected of being disabled as handouts or on overheads and discuss the various components of the evaluation.

4. Bring to class the Vineland Adaptive Behavior Scale or another measure for the students' perusal and discussion.

5. Invite any person with a disability to class as a guest speaker. They could discuss the disability and its impact on daily life as well as experiences with the psychological assessment process. Encourage questions from the class. The on-campus director of disability concerns can be an excellent source of the names of students with disabilities who might be willing to serve as guest speakers in your class.

SUGGESTED ASSIGNMENTS

1. Each student chooses one of the assessment methods or adaptations of standardized instruments discussed in Chapter 16. Students then locate and summarize in writing current reviews of their test in reference books such as the *Mental Measurements Yearbook*. For students enrolled or planning to enroll in a special education curriculum, selection of tests can be based on the type of exceptionality with which they plan to work.

2. Groups of students can interview appropriate school personnel (e.g., directors of special education, school psychologists) regarding the types of programs available in their districts for students with various types of disabilities and methods used for identification. If the school psychologist is interviewed, specific discussion can focus on the types of modifications in test administration procedures that are used with various types of exceptional students as well as examples of tests used that are designed for a specific type of exceptionality. Issues related to the appropriateness of normative comparisons with disabled or nondisabled individuals can also be discussed. The issue of legal requirements for the evaluation of students with disabilities should also be addressed. Subsequent class discussion can focus on what information the students were able to obtain during their interviews.

3. Students can also interview the director of disability concerns on their college campus to obtain information about the types of services available to college students with disabilities and methods of determining eligibility for these services.

MEDIA RESOURCES

Assessing a Young Child (1974, OKentU, 25 minutes, color). Demonstrates the assessment of mentally handicapped children age eight and under. Includes assessment of physical, behavioral, and developmental capacities to determine educational needs.

Assessment: Physically Challenged (1985, PBS, 30 minutes, color, VHS). Video presents a discussion of how to accurately evaluate a young child (birth to age five) who is physically challenged to assess development and develop an appropriate intervention program.

Cognitive Development (1985, PBS, 30 minutes, color, VHS). Video presents the principles of cognitive development and the effects of disabling conditions on cognitive skills. Teachers demonstrate techniques and strategies to promote cognitive growth with infants, toddlers, and preschoolers.

The Evaluation by the School Psychologist (1977, PSt, 20 minutes, color). Demonstrates the entire psychological assessment process (from initial parental consent to final case staffing conference) for a student referred for a psychological evaluation by his classroom teacher due to a learning problem.

IQ—Questionable Criterion (1967, AzU, 13 minutes, color/b&w). Recommends the use of a more comprehensive evaluation than just an IQ test to diagnose mental retardation.

Learning Disabilities (FHS, 19 minutes, color, VHS). Examines this frequently misdiagnosed and misunderstood condition. Stresses the importance of early diagnosis and intervention. A nine-year-old boy is depicted.

Testing Multiply Handicapped Children (1963, FTS, 30 minutes, color/b&w). Demonstrates modifications of test material and other techniques used to assess children with multiple handicaps including motor impairments and the deaf/blind.

Testing Multiply Handicapped Children. Part I: Kevin—A 6-Year-Old with Cerebral Palsy (1963, FTS, 30 minutes, b&w). Provides a more detailed (compared to the film above) description of the psychological evaluation of a six-year-old with cerebral palsy.

The End Is My Beginning: An Interdisciplinary Approach to the Assessment of Developmentally Delayed Children (1981, BC, 40 minutes, color, VHS). Explains and demonstrates a multidisciplinary approach to diagnosis and treatment of children with developmental disabilities.

Where to Begin with Nonverbal Children (1974, PSt, 17 minutes, color). Demonstrates one technique for informal screening/assessing children who are nonverbal. Five children (one without and four with speech problems) are depicted in the film.

REFERENCES

Carroll, J. L. (1974). Demonstrating techniques simulating four learning disabilities. *Journal of Learning Disabilities, 5,* 287–289.

McCallum, L. W. (1979). Experiences for understanding exceptional children. *Teaching of Psychology, 6,* 118–119.

CHAPTER 17

Industrial/Organizational Assessment

CLASS DISCUSSION QUESTIONS

Much of this chapter is concerned with preemployment counseling and personnel psychology. A logical approach to this material might entail references to adages such as the one about "getting the right person for the right job" or not "trying to fit a square peg into a round hole." In specific detail, what elements of the job and the person for the job must mesh for the chances of a satisfactory outcome to be good? What is the role of variables such as interest, aptitude, and personality? Students may be encouraged to come up with job descriptions as well as personality descriptions and be prepared to explain why certain personality types would and would not "fit" into a particular employment situation.

Other potential class discussion questions are as follows:

1. Share your experiences with any of the tests discussed in this chapter such as vocational interest and aptitude tests used as part of the vocational guidance process.

2. Has any class member been in an employment situation that has used portfolio, performance, or physical tests in the selection process? The instructor can share personal experiences relating to these assessment approaches and if they are used in the selection or evaluation process for college professors in their department.

3. As a follow-up to the Everyday Psychometrics section, inquire if any member of the class has ever been administered this test. For what purposes and how were the results used? Based on the reliability and validity data reviewed in the text, what conclusions can be made about the reliability and validity of the test and what implications does this data have for using the test in the employment or academic setting?

4. Have any class members had experience with an assessment center? If so, ask them to describe their experiences.

5. What method was used to construct the Strong Interest Inventory? Has it "kept up with the times"? Have any students had experience with this test? If so, ask them to share their reactions and how the test results were used.

6. As a follow-up to the chapter Close-Up, Validity Generalization and the GATB, discuss the concept of "validity generalization" and how it relates to personnel selection. What are its implications for personnel directors? The implications for society at large?

7. Differentiate the terms "selection," "classification," and "placement." What types of measurement instruments are used as part of each of these functions? Give specific examples of each term.

8. Have any students had any experience with application blanks? Did they meet the criteria specified in the chapter?

9. Discuss the advantages and limitations of letters of recommendation. Discuss how they have been used in employee selection for jobs students have applied for. What screening approaches have been combined with letters of recommendation?

10. Divide students into smaller discussion groups and ask them to develop performance samples for jobs other than those discussed in the chapter—for example, college instructor, clerk at the student bookstore, food service worker, department office secretary. Students can select jobs in which they are currently employed. What approaches would they recommend for screening, classification, and placement of workers for these positions? Would they make use of drug testing and integrity tests? If so, based on the cases presented in the text, would their use be legal?

11. Review, as a class, the cases presented in Chapter 17. Discussion can include reactions to the types of height and weight standards that have been challenged, those that have been found inappropriate and those upheld. Do students agree with the courts? Discuss the issue of race norming and its legality. Discuss implications of race norming or the lack of it for society at large.

12. How can personality tests complement the use of aptitude and interest inventories (in personnel and career decision making)?

13. Why are measures of aptitude (e.g., GATB) important in career and personnel decisions? How are they used? How can they be most effective and useful?

14. What types of gender differences have been found in large-scale studies of particular vocational interest and aptitude inventories/tests? Do these differences challenge the reliability and validity of the tests? Do they raise the issue of whether or not the tests are biased? Encourage students to refer back to previous discussions of test bias in the course.

15. Discuss the relationship between motivation, attitude, and productivity. Why are I/O psychologists interested in these constructs? Describe assessment approaches for job satisfaction, organizational commitment, and organizational culture.

16. What is the reliability and validity evidence for "integrity tests"? Have any students taken a drug test and/or integrity tests? How were the tests conducted, and what were reactions to this practice? Discuss issues related to the reliability and validity of this practice.

17. What are the different approaches to managerial selection? What does the research suggest about factors that influence the decision to employ an individual at the managerial level?

18. Discuss the concept of race norming. What are the advantages and limitations of this concept?

19. Discuss the mandates relating to the application process that are included in the Americans with Disabilities Act of 1990.

CLASS DEMONSTRATIONS

1. An industrial/organizational psychologist could be invited to class as a guest speaker. The talk might focus on how I/O psychologists use measurement principles and tests in their work. Students can read the chapter prior to the talk and be encouraged to ask questions relating to concepts presented in the text.

2. A colleague on the faculty with expertise in the use of the Strong Interest Inventory and/or the Myers-Briggs Type Indicator can be invited to speak to the class about this test(s). The focus of the talk can be on the uses of the test and its technical characteristics. A good resource is often an I/O or counseling psychologist.

3. Students in the class can take the Strong Interest Inventory and comment on the administration and interpretation provided.

4. Invite as guest speakers a guidance counselor from the local high school and a vocational counselor from your on-campus student counseling center. The topic of their talk could be the use of tests in the vocational guidance process. Both interest and aptitude tests should be addressed in their talks.

5. Invite a personnel director to speak on the use of tests and other methods (e.g., application blank, references, interview) in the personnel selection/retention process. Questions should also be posed regarding the implications of the concept of validity generalization.

6. Invite a lawyer, specializing in employment discrimination litigation, to speak to your class on the types of cases typically brought to litigation. The focus of the discussion might be on what types of personnel selection/retention methods (particularly tests) have been most commonly challenged in the courts.

7. Invite your university/college affirmative action officer to be a guest speaker. Her talk can focus on how her office impacts on the selection process for positions in the university. Ask her to comment on the issue of race norming and separate gender norms.

8. An engineering psychologist might be invited to class as a guest speaker. The talk can center around the field of engineering psychology and the use of measurement theory and methods.

9. Administer an integrity test to the entire class. Discussion can follow on reactions to the administration and issues related to its reliability and validity.

10. An employment counselor based in your local office of the state department of vocational rehabilitation services can be invited to speak. He or she could address how tests are used for vocational placement and how the Americans with Disabilities Act of 1990 is being implemented in your state.

11. If a large corporation is located in your community, invite the I/O psychologist to speak to your class. Ask him or her to address the issue of if and how the employees' level of corporate commitment and perceptions of the organizational culture are assessed in their organization. Also ask the guest speaker to comment on the use of tests to measure personal integrity and drug use as well as other aspects of their employee selection and retention process.

SUGGESTED ASSIGNMENTS

1. Assign one or more students to visit the state employment service and register to take the General Aptitude Test Battery. Encourage them to share their experiences with the test with the rest of the class.

2. Assign students to visit local businesses and obtain application blanks. Then ask them to critique the application form using the criteria specified in the chapter. For students visiting large department stores, they can also inquire how/if drug testing and/or integrity tests are used in their employee selection process. What laws/court cases have impacted their use?

3. Instruct students to look up a test related to "vocations" in the *Mental Measurements Yearbook* and prepare a written critique. Critiques can be shared with the rest of the class and integrated with material presented in the text.

4. Divide your class into two groups to form a panel debate. One group would be a proponent for the use of validity generalization in personnel selection; the other group would oppose the use of validity generalization in personnel selection. Topics to be debated should include the use of meta-analytic statistical procedures, among other topics related to validity generalization. Students would consult the relevant literature to provide support for their position.

5. An alternative to the panel debate format in the preceding assignment would consist of having each student prepare a written report that considers both the pros and cons of validity generalization in personnel selection. After the detailing of both the pros and cons (summarized from a review of the relevant literature), each student would then state his/her own personal opinions concerning the use of validity generalization.

6. Divide students into groups and assign them to visit local high school guidance counselors to discuss with them what tests they use in the vocational guidance process. These tests would include both interest and aptitude. Representatives from each of the groups would then report back to the whole class.

7. Students can prepare a paper discussing the types of gender differences that have been found in large-scale studies of vocational interest and aptitude inventories/tests. The students can take a position on whether or not these differences challenge the reliability and validity of the tests and if they raise the issue of whether or not the tests are biased. Encourage students to refer back to previous discussions of test bias in the course.

8. Divide students into two groups to discuss the pros and cons of integrity testing and drug testing. They should investigate resources cited in the chapter to prepare for this "debate."

MEDIA RESOURCES

A Dialogue on Vocational Development Theory: John Holland and Donald Super (APGA, 40 minutes, color). Discussion by two prominent theorists discussing their contributions to vocational development theory. Drs. Holland and Super also address similarities and differences between their theories and the essential issues in career development.

The Americans with Disabilities Act (ADA): New Access to the Workplace (1991, UMN, 39 minutes, color, VHS). Explains the ADA, which bans discrimination against people with disabilities by employers. Dramatizes the handling of hiring and employment issues that may be encountered.

Assessing Employee Potential (1972, ED&MGT, 63 minutes, color, VHS). Problems of assessing and developing the potential of employees are considered. Modules include general problems in assessing employees, matching people and positions, assessment methods including on-the-job assessment and the assessment center.

Assessment Center (1987, DJA, 33 minutes, VHS). Assessment center participants involved in several exercises are observed.

Assessment Centers (1985, DJA, 50 minutes, color, VHS). The program discusses how and why assessment centers work for managerial hiring and promotion decisions.

A New Look at Motivation (1980, CRM/McH, 32 minutes, color). Discussion by David McClelland related to how the needs for affiliation, power, and achievement motivate people's actions. Also illustrates how employees differ in their motivational needs and discusses effective ways to increase the motivation of employees of various personality types.

Common Sense Motivation (RdT, 12 minutes, color). Discusses the sources of job satisfaction that motivate employees.

Interviewing Techniques—The Face-to-Face Interview (1983, PMA, 59 minutes, color, VHS). Discusses and demonstrates interviewing for selection.

The Interview Film: What to Know and What to Do (1977, IU, 21 minutes, color). Illustrates and discusses the entire interviewing process from initial inquiries to the interviewer's screening, evaluation, and final decision.

Matching Job Types with Personality Types (RMI, 30 minutes, color, VHS). Discusses how to match unique personality types with the right career.

More Than Just a Gut Feeling (1984, AmM, 29 minutes, b&w). Demonstrates behavioral interviewing.

Motivation: Classic Concepts (1987, CRM, 21 minutes, color, film and VHS). Demonstrates to managers how to motivate employees to their full potential by addressing their needs, aspirations, and values. Five classic motivational theories identify the factors that motivate different people.

No Two Alike (1962, UofMN, 30 minutes, b&w). Dr. Lloyd Humphries discusses how tests were developed for selecting pilots for WWII. Dr. James Gallagher demonstrates methods being used to develop creative thinking in the classroom.

Performance Appraisal: The Human Dynamics (1978, PSt, 25 minutes, color). Reviews the purposes and methods of performance appraisal.

Personnel (FHS, 31 minutes, color, VHS). Addresses the issues of finding, training, motivating, compensating, and retaining good employees. Included is a discussion of how to conduct a selection interview and how to utilize information from the interview and the resume in employee selection.

CHAPTER 18

Consumer Assessment

CLASS DISCUSSION QUESTIONS

As a means of entering the world of consumer psychology, why not try your hand at conducting a "mini" focus group? Videotape a television commercial, or simply clip a print ad and bring it to this class session. Now you are the moderator and your class is the group of respondents; you'll want to probe what the group is thinking and feeling about the ad and exactly what effect the ad appears to be having. For example, if it's a television commercial for a soft drink, are the people pictured in the commercial the kind of people the students would like to have a soft drink with? If it's a radio commercial, do the students think it would have the "stopping power" to break through the clutter of commercials on the radio and make them stop and listen? What about a print ad; if they saw it in the newspaper or magazine, would they attend to it or just keep turning pages? And most important, this exercise should stimulate some class discussion as to (1) *why* advertising works or fails to work, and (2) the methods by which the success or failure of advertising can best be assessed.

Other potential class discussion questions are as follows:

1. How does the measurement of attitudes in consumer psychology compare/contrast with the measurement of attitudes in clinical, counseling, educational, and personnel psychology? How are they similar? How are they different? Students should cite specific examples of each.

2. What tools are used in research on consumer behavior? What measurement principles/issues must be kept in mind?

3. Discuss the different types of scaling techniques and the advantages and limitations of each.

4. Discuss any personal experiences you've had with any of the tools of marketing research discussed in the chapter (e.g., mall intercept, mail or telephone interviews, focus groups, in-depth interviews, psychophysiological measures, projective techniques). What were your impressions of the methods from a psychometric point of view (e.g., was it a good or poor survey)? How might it have been improved?

5. What's a focus group? Discuss its advantages and disadvantages for consumer assessment.

6. How are projective techniques used in consumer research?

7. Compare and contrast the three different types of survey techniques: face-to-face, telephone, and mail. What are the advantages and disadvantages of each? What specific factors might make one technique more appropriate than another? Cite examples.

8. Discuss the use of psychophysiological measures in consumer research. Compare their use in this context with their use as presented in Chapter 13.

9. As a follow-up to the Everyday Psychometrics section, discuss the similarities and differences of adaptive testing in intellectual assessment and in consumer assessment. Give examples of each.

10. As a follow-up to the chapter Close-Up, discuss the value of assessing brand equity in consumer research. Outline the steps in this type of assessment.

11. As a part-time job, have any students had any experience with consumer assessments by conducting telephone surveys or face-to-face interviews? If so, ask them to share their experiences.

CLASS DEMONSTRATIONS

1. Invite to class as a guest speaker a consumer psychologist and/or a marketing specialist who specializes in consumer psychology. Ask your guest to focus his or her talk on the various methods/instruments used in this area and the implications of various psychometric issues (e.g., reliability and validity, sampling procedures). If you do not personally know a consumer psychologist, you may wish to contact Division 23 (Consumer Psychology) of the American Psychological Association for a referral. If a psychologist specializing in consumer psychology is not available in your area, you might also consider asking a representative from a marketing firm that might be based locally.

2. Invite an aide to a local state politician (senator or representative) to be a guest speaker for the class. The speaker could address the issues of how surveys to constituents are constructed and developed, and why they are important. He or she could bring examples to class. Questions would focus on the psychometric adequacy of the surveys and sampling procedures. How is this form of assessment related to the topic of consumer assessment?

SUGGESTED ASSIGNMENTS

1. Groups of students can interview personnel in the marketing departments of local business and industry or individuals associated with marketing research companies. The interview can center

around the types of methods used in the area and the implications of psychometric issues such as reliability, validity, and sampling. Students can prepare a written report of their efforts and also report to the class.

2. Students are assigned the task of looking up a test related to consumer assessment in the *Mental Measurements Yearbook* and then writing a critique. They should include in the critique a section integrating the information presented with the concepts discussed in the chapter.

3. Ask students to review recent magazines and newspapers and choose an advertisement to analyze. The analysis, which could be conducted in groups during class time, would include discussing the various aspects of the advertisement related to consumer psychology that are discussed in the chapter (e.g., positioning of the product, motivation of the consumer).

4. Assign students to groups and instruct them to choose a product for which they will assess consumer attitudes. The assignment, using the concepts presented in the chapter, is to construct an attitude survey. Class discussion of the survey, led by the group that constructed it, would include an analysis of the survey based on the material presented in the text; for example: What type of scale was chosen? Why? How will a sample be selected? What type of sample?

5. As in the exercise presented in Chapter 18, readers are asked to approach a person they know who wears Coca-Cola (or another brand name) clothing and conduct an in-depth interview. The interview will attempt to assess what motivates the person to buy such clothing. Impressions, based on the interview, can be shared during class discussion.

6. Have students contact local malls or shopping centers to determine if any focus groups are held there. If so, the class is encouraged to observe. Subsequent discussion can focus on an evaluation of the method from a psychometric point of view.

7. Divide the students into groups of two to four. Tell each group that they have been hired by Mayfield Publishing Company to develop a survey assessing students' opinions about their *Psychological Testing and Assessment* textbook. The groups must decide if the survey will be face-to-face, telephone, or by mail; they must decide on the scaling method they will use (aggregate, multidimensional, or semantic differential); and finally they must decide on the content of the survey and write a rough draft of it. Each group can then critique another group's rough draft and send the survey back to the original group for revision. The "best" survey determined by a class vote can be administered to the class with the results forwarded to the authors, care of Mayfield Publishing Company.

MEDIA RESOURCES

Consumer Behavior I (RMI, 30 minutes, color, VHS). Introduces the forces that influence individual consumer behavior.

Consumer Behavior II (RMI, 30 minutes, color, VHS). Explores how marketing specialists gain an understanding of consumers and of what motivates the consumer to buy.

CHAPTER 19

Computer-Assisted Psychological Assessment

CLASS DISCUSSION QUESTIONS

This chapter deals with the topic of computer-assisted psychological assessment (CAPA) and herein lies the basis for an initial discussion on pencil-and-paper versus computerized test administration. Many of the students will have had experience as a testtaker on a computer; having them share their experiences in terms of the contrast between the different ways a test can be taken may be instructive. This may be followed by a discussion of computerized testtaking from the perspective of the examiner—including all the pros, cons, and ethical dilemmas inherent in such procedures.

Other potential class discussion questions are as follows:

1. Compare and contrast CAPA and CATI. Discuss the advantages and limitations of CATI.

2. What are the advantages and disadvantages of CAPA? What concerns have been raised concerning the practice?

3. What are ways in which computer-adaptive testing can enhance the reliability and validity of test results?

4. Discuss the various uses of item-branching technology. Encourage students to think of their experience with commonly administered tests (e.g., GRE, ACT, U.S. Constitution test, driver's license test, visual and hearing acuity tests) and how this technology could be helpful in the development and administration of these tests.

5. Discuss the "confession/computer hypothesis." Ask students to comment on whether or not they would be more inclined to reveal personal information to a computer as compared to a "live" clinician.

6. The authors point out in Chapter 19 that currently no government regulations exist for CAPA-related publishing or traditional psychological test publishing. Do your students believe that government regulations should be developed to control the CAPA-related publishing and/or traditional psychological test publishing?

7. Who should be allowed access to CAPA-related products?

8. Are the SAT and GRE considered computer-assisted? Why or why not? Have students discuss if they have had experience taking the SAT or GRE by computer.

9. Comment on whether or not you (the instructor) have developed an "item bank" for this course. Why or why not?

10. Can scores on a conventionally administered test be considered equivalent to scores on a computer-assisted administration of the same test? Why or why not? Consider areas such as effects of item type, item content, and the testtakers' attitudes and emotional reactions.

11. Relating to inputting of tests, compare and contrast central processing, teleprocessing, and local processing. Review the advantages and limitations of each.

12. Compare and contrast simple versus extended scoring, descriptive, screening, and consultative reports. Bring in examples to illustrate each (see demonstration #1).

13. Review the suggested questions to be raised when a psychologist is considering the use of a computer-administered version of a conventional test. Direct the students' attention to Table 19–1.

14. Discuss the relationship between the Barnum effect and the validity of CAPA personality inventories.

15. As a follow-up to the Everyday Psychometrics section, discuss the advantages and disadvantages of a system such as the Treatment/Evaluation Manager-2000 or TEM-2000. As an employee of a mental health facility, would you favor the use of such a system? Why or why not? As a client, would you favor its use? Why or why not? What ethical issues are raised by the use of such a system?

CLASS DEMONSTRATIONS

1. Arrange to obtain copies of various computer-assisted psychological and/or educational test scoring and interpretation software. If you cannot locate one in your department or student counseling center, write to a publisher (Psychological Corporation or American Guidance Service). One or more of these programs can be demonstrated to the class by bringing a PC to class or meeting in the university/college computer lab. If this is not possible, the instructor can prepare handouts of the computer-generated output (reprinted CATI reports are included in *101 Exercises in Psychological*

Testing and Assessment, Third Edition). Try to provide examples of the different types of scoring and interpretive reports (i.e., simple scoring reports, extended scoring reports, and various types of interpretive reports). Subsequent discussion can focus on reacting to the issues presented in the chapter.

2. Write for a copy of the APA's *Guidelines for Computer-Based Interpretation and Assessment* and share it with the class for further discussion and elaboration. Various other groups of psychologists have developed similar guidelines (e.g., National Association of School Psychologists, 4340 East West Highway, Suite 402, Bethesda, MD 20814).

3. Bring to class the APA's *Standards for Educational and Psychological Tests and Manuals and Ethical Principles for Psychologists* for further elaboration and discussion of the use of computer in psychological assessment.

4. Contact a large corporation based locally and inquire whether or not they use any forms of computerized adaptive testing. If so, invite a representative of their personnel department to speak to the class. His or her talk can focus on describing the process and its perceived strengths and limitations.

5. Contact your local school system(s) and determine if any teachers are using programs such as Make-A-Test or Create-A-Test. Invite users to class to discuss their impressions.

6. Invite to class as a guest speaker a clinical or counseling psychologist who uses computer-assisted psychological assessment for test administration, scoring, and/or interpretation. Encourage the speaker to share specific examples of how she/he uses the computer.

7. Share with the class your item bank—not the specific questions but rather by which variables you have items classified.

8. Write to the Educational Testing Service in Princeton, New Jersey, and request information on how they develop item banks for their standardized tests.

SUGGESTED ASSIGNMENTS

1. Assign students to one of two groups—a pro and a con side to the issue of computer-based psychological assessment including computer-based test administration. Each group spends time researching its position, culminating in an in-class "debate" of the issues.

2. Students can choose one of the issues (e.g., computer-assisted test administration, interpretation) presented in Chapter 19 that particularly interests them. Their assignment would be to prepare a short written report and oral presentation to the class after researching their topic.

3. Using a computer database, have students locate one article on the topic of CAPA or CATI and summarize its contents. Class discussion can focus on relating the topic to information presented in the chapter or class.

4. Divide the class into three or four groups. Have each group create an item bank for the Association of Personal Trainers Who Make House Calls (APTHC) certification examination and then present their bank to the class. Each group should respond to the questions listed in Table 1 of the chapter Close-Up, Designing an Item Bank.

APPENDIX

SUPPLIERS OF MEDIA RESOURCES

AAVP   Access Audio/Video Productions
P. O. Box 5547
Berkeley, CA 94705

AIC   Curtis Blake Center
American International College
100 State Street
Springfield, MA 01109

AIM   Association Instructional Materials
866 Third Avenue
New York, NY 10022

AIT   Agency for Instructional Technology
111 West 17th Street, Box A
Bloomington, IN 47402

AmM   American Media, Inc.
4900 University Avenue, Suite 100
West Des Moines, IA 50266-6769

APA   American Psychological Association
Continuing Education Department
750 First Street, N.E.
Washington, DC 20002

APGA   APGA Film Sales
607 New Hampshire Avenue, N.W.
Washington, DC 20002

AW   Addison-Wesley Testing Service
South Street
Reading, MA 01867

AzU   University of Arizona
Video Campus
Marvill Building, No. 76, Box 4
Tucson, AZ 85721

BC   Biomedical Communications
University of Arizona
Arizona Health Services Center
Tucson, AZ 85724

CAM 3   CAM 3 Associates
5101 Chapman Highway
Knoxville, TN 37920

COM   Concept Media
P.O. Box 19542
Irvine, CA 92714

CRM/McH   CRM/McGraw-Hill
P.O. Box 641
Del Mar, CA 92014

CLU   University of California/Los Angeles
Instructional Media Library
Powell Library, Room 46
Los Angeles, CA 90024

CoU   University of Colorado
Academic Services
Box 379
Boulder, CO 80309

CtU   University of Connecticut
Center for Inst. Media & Technology
Storrs, CT 06268

CU   University of California
Extension Media Center
2176 Shattuck
Berkeley, CA 94704

DF   Davidson Films, Inc.
231 East Street
Davis, CA 95616

DJA   Dennis A. Joiner and Associates
4975 Daru Way
Fair Oakes, CA 95628-5452

ED&MGT   Resources for Education and
Management, Inc.
1804 Montreal Court, Suite A
Tucker, GA 30084

ETS   Educational Testing Service
Princeton, NJ 08540

FAV   Fairview Audio-Visuals
Division of Health Cleveland
Enterprises, Inc.
1709 Groveland Avenue
Cleveland, OH 44111

FHS   Films for the Humanities and Sciences
            Video Divisions: FFH Video
            Box 2053
            Princeton, NJ 08543-2053

FTaSU   Florida State University
            Instructional Support Center
            Film Library
            54 Johnston Bldg.
            Tallahasse, FL 32306

FTS   University of South Florida
            Film Library
            4202 Fowler Ave.
            Tampa, FL 33620

HRM   HRM Video
            175 Tompkins Avenue
            No. V212
            Pleasantville, NY 10570-0839

HS   Hubbard Scientific
            1120 Halbleib Road
            Chippewa Falls, WI 54729

IaAS   Iowa State University
            Media Resource Center
            121 Pearson Hall
            Ames, IA 50011

IaU   University of Iowa
            Audio-Visual Center
            C-215 Seashore Hall
            Iowa City, IA 52242

ICarbS   Southern Illinois University
            Learning Resources Center
            Carbondale, IL 62901

InLP   Purdue University
            Cooperative Extension Service
            Media Distribution Center
            301 South Second Street
            Lafayette, IN 47905

InTI   Indiana State University
            Audio Visual Center
            Stalker Hall
            Terre Haute, IN 47807

ITS   International Telecommunications
               Services
            P.O. Box 1290
            State College, PA 16804

IU   University of Illinois Film Center
            1325 Oak Street
            Champaign, IL 61820

InU   Indiana University
            Audio-Visual Center
            Bloomington, IN 47405

JF   Journal Films and Video Inc.
            5160 Sherman Avenue, Suite 100
            Evanston, IL 60201

KU   University of Kansas
            Film Rental Library
            Continuing Education Library
            Lawrence, KS 66045

MS   Magna Systems, Inc.
            West County Line 95
            Barrington, IL 60010

MBU   Boston University
            Krasker Memorial Film Library
            565 Commonwealth Ave.
            Boston, MA 02215

McH   Contemporary Films, Inc.
            McGraw-Hill Book Co.
            1221 Ave. of the Americas
            New York, NY 10020

MiDW   Wayne State University
            Media Services
            5265 Cass Avenue
            Detroit, MI 48202

MiU   University of Michigan
            Michigan Media
            400 Fourth Street
            Ann Arbor, MI 48103-4816

UMN   University of Minnesota
            Media Distribution
            Box 734, Mayo Memorial Building
            420 Delaware Street SE
            Minneapolis, MN 55455

MOU   University of Missouri/Columbia
            Film Library
            505 E. Stewart Rd.
            Columbia, MO 65211

NASP   National Association of
School Psychologists
4340 East West Highway, Suite 402
Bethesda, MD 20814

NCME   National Council on Measurement
in Education
ATTN: J.C.P.
1230 Seventeenth Street, N.W.
Washington, DC 20036-3078

NSyU   Syracuse University
Film Rental Center
1455 E. Colvin St.
Syracuse, NY 13210

OKentU   Kent State University
Audio-Visual Services
330 Library Bldg.
Kent, OH 44242

PBS   Division of Public Broadcasting
Service
1320 Braddock Place
Alexandria, VA 22314-1698

PMA   Paul Mok & Assaociates
14455 Webb Chapel Road
Dallas, TX 78713

PPiU   University of Pittsburgh
Media Services
G-20 Hillman Library
Pittsburgh, PA 15260

PSt   Pennsylvania State University
Audio-Visual Services
Special Services Building
1127 Fox Hill Road
State College, PA 16803-1824

Psy. Corp   Psychological Corporation
Order Service Center
P.O. Box 839954
San Antonio, TX 78283-3954

RdT   Roundtable Films
113 North San Vincente Blvd.
Beverly Hills, CA 90211

RivP   Riverside Publishing Co.
8420 Bryn Mawr
Chicago, IL 60631

RMI   RMI Media Productions, Inc.
1365 North Winchester
Olathe, Kansas 66061

TxU   University of Texas at Austin
General Libraries
Film Library
Box W
Austin, TX 78713

VLRG   Videolearning Resource Group
354 West Lancaster Avenue
Haverford, PA 19041

WaEIC   Central Washington University
Media Library Services
IMC
Ellensburg, WA 98926

WU   University of Wisconsin/Madison
Bureau of Audio-Visual Instruction
1327 University Ave.
P.O. Box 2093
Madison, WI 53701

Instructor's Manual to Accompany

101 Exercises in Psychological Testing and Assessment

Third Edition

Ronald Jay Cohen
St. John's University

Prepared by

Ronald Jay Cohen
Suzanne M. Phillips
Mark E. Swerdlik

TO THE INSTRUCTOR

101 Exercises in Psychological Testing and Assessment, in its third edition, is a companion book to be used either as a supplement to *Psychological Testing and Assessment: An Introduction to Tests and Measurement* (Cohen, Swerdlik, & Phillips, 1996) or in conjunction with other psychological testing texts used for courses variously described as "psychological testing," "psychological assessment," and "tests and measurement." It was created to supplement textbook study and in-class lecture material with hands-on laboratory exercises.

Each chapter of *101 Exercises* contains two or more exercises, some of which can be completed in-class during a laboratory period and some of which require out-of-class execution and/or preparation. Some of the exercises require collaborative effort whereas others can be completed independently. All of the exercises require application of learning, and many call upon the student to think critically and/or respond creatively. It will be up to you to decide which exercise to assign depending on your particular course objectives. Part 1 of this section of the *Instructor's Manual* briefly describes all of the exercises. Part 2 contains answers to selected exercises.

We hope that you find the third edition of *101 Exercises in Psychological Testing and Assessment* helpful in assisting your students in mastering course objectives and in helping to make the field of psychological measurement more exciting and personally meaningful to them.

Part 1
A Description of the Exercises

CHAPTER 1

PSYCHOLOGICAL TESTING AND ASSESSMENT

Exercise #1
ON MEASUREMENT

Students write a brief essay on the subject of measurement. Students are asked to discuss their thoughts on the subject of measurement in general—and their essays need not relate directly to measurement in psychology. They can choose either a formal paper well-researched with references to the scholarly literature or a more informal, free-wheeling, even humorous paper. A sample essay is presented dealing with the early history of measurement.

Exercise #2
TESTING OR ASSESSMENT

In an effort to illustrate that the semantic difference between psychological testing and psychological assessment is not always straightforward, students are given the task of classifying various activities as either "testing" or "assessment." The exercise compels the student to think about these two important concepts and to think about how they differ.

Exercise #3
THE PROCESS OF ASSESSMENT

Students role-play an independent distributor of "Cramway," an herbal product designed to lessen test anxiety. Students respond to the following questions: (1) Which tools of assessment (test, interview, case study, etc.) will be selected for use in an outcome study? (2) What are the rights and responsibilities of the parties in the assessment process? (3) According to library references used as sources of information about tests, which measure of anxiety would be best to use in the study?

Exercise #4
THE INTERVIEWER/INTERVIEWEE INTERACTION

This represents an in-class exercise that entails various class members playing the roles of interviewer and interviewee while the rest of the class is instructed to note differences in interviewing styles.

Exercise #5
BEHAVIORAL ASSESSMENT

Students are given background information related to the need for staff of community-based facilities for developmentally disabled children and adults, to monitor progress necessary for independent living. After studying an example of a behavioral programming scale for one such independent living skill, "Emptying Garbage Scale," students are asked to create their own scale. They are asked to develop their scale by taking some relatively simple behavior necessary for independent living, and then break it up into its component behaviors.

Exercise #6
GETTING INFORMATION ABOUT TESTS

In the role of a psychologist employed at a university counseling center, it is the task of the student to advise the dean about the appropriateness of using the Minnesota Multiphasic Personality Inventory-2 (MMPI-2) as a screening device for personnel to be employed at a child day-care center. The student's task is to gather relevant information on the MMPI-2 from all available sources and then report back.

CHAPTER 2

HISTORICAL, CULTURAL, AND LEGAL/ETHICAL CONSIDERATIONS

Exercise #7
PSYCHOLOGICAL TESTING AND ASSESSMENT IN HISTORICAL PERSPECTIVE

The student is challenged to think of (a) how psychological tests could be brought to bear on three important questions facing society today, and (b) how comparable issues might have been dealt with in societies of the past in which there was an absence of psychological tests.

Exercise #8
THE COHEN CHICKEN SOUP ESSAY

In an effort to illustrate the importance and need for cultural sensitivity in test development, a panel of three students acting as judges is appointed. The rest of the entire class, or small groups within it, holds a "Chicken Soup Challenge." Each participant writes down his or her recipe for chicken soup. The panel of judges will select the best recipe. A spokesperson for the judging panel is asked to explain why the winning recipe won, likely making reference to their own preferences based on culture. Losing participants then debate with the judges why their submissions did not win top honors. The task for the entire class is to develop a set of culturally sensitive rules for judging essays in future contests.

Exercise #9
THE NONVERBAL INTERVIEW

In an effort to illustrate the role of nonverbal behavior during an interview, students team up in pairs and role-play an interviewer and interviewee with the choice of context of the interview (e.g., physician-patient, psychologist-client, news reporter-interviewee, etc.) decided by each group and each dyad then prepares in advance a list of interview questions. The questions should lend themselves to nonverbal as well as verbal responses. The team is asked to prepare in advance a list of the nonverbal answers that the interviewee will be trying to convey in responses to each of the questions. Volunteer dyads will perform their interviews before the whole class. The task for the entire class, after each role-play, is to guess the nonverbal response to each of the questions followed by a discussion of the role of nonverbal behavior during the interview.

Exercise #10
GUIDELINES FOR USING PSYCHOLOGICAL TESTS

From their own background and experience, students are challenged to compile a list of commonsense guidelines that they believe should apply in areas ranging from test development through test use and interpretation.

Exercise #11
THE TEST PURCHASER QUALIFICATION FORM

Students are assigned the task of designing a "Uniform Psychological Test Purchase Qualification Form" to be used by all publishers of psychological tests. Students are also asked to explain the rationale for requiring such information from the test purchaser prior to selling the test.

Exercise #12
A LEGAL/ETHICAL ROUNDTABLE

The scenario for this in-class roundtable is that all students are members of the State Board for Psychology. The board is meeting to come to some resolution regarding outstanding issues pertaining to areas such as minimal requirements for test standardization, test manuals, and test use. How should rules regarding the purchase and/or use of psychological tests be enforced? What rights should be listed under the "Testtaker's Bill of Rights"? These are but some of the questions and issues that may be tackled by the board.

Exercise #13
ANOTHER LEGAL/ETHICAL ROUNDTABLE

This exercise represents a continuation of Exercise #12 except that the focus here is on issues of malpractice and professional liability. Synopses of six actual cases are read to the board members as a stimulus for discussion of the pertinent legal/ethical issues.

CHAPTER 3

A STATISTICS REFRESHER

Exercise #14
SCALES OF MEASUREMENT IN EVERYDAY LIFE

Examples of scales of measurement (nominal, ordinal, interval, and ratio) found in everyday life are presented. Students are then asked to provide their own additional examples of each of the four types of scales and why each example selected is classified as that particular type of measurement.

Exercise #15
REVIEWING DESCRIPTIVE STATISTICS

Using the raw scores on a hypothetical 100-item, multiple-choice test administered to 25 students, the calculation of measures of central tendency and variability are illustrated in step-by-step fashion. Then students are called upon to graphically illustrate other data (height in inches of class members) as well as calculate measures of central tendency and variability.

Exercise #16
ACCUMULATING DATA ON A MOCK PERSONALITY INVENTORY

Students administer a mock personality test (Mid-Pawling Personality Inventory, MPPI) found in Appendix A of *101 Exercises* to a fellow student, the data of which will be used in forthcoming exercises.

CHAPTER 4

NORMS, CORRELATION, AND REGRESSION

Exercise #17
TRANSFORMED SCORES: PERCENTILES

This exercise contains Harold Seashore's article, "Methods of Expressing Test Scores," as a prelude to discussion and exercises having to do with this topic. Using data from a hypothetical distribution of scores, students are asked to convert five raw scores into percentiles. A 10-item true/false test on percentiles concludes the chapter (see page 121 for the answer key to this test).

Exercise #18
STANDARD, STANDARDIZED, AND NORMALIZED STANDARD SCORES

After a brief refresher on the computation of standard scores, students are asked to answer questions about them with reference to a graph of a normal curve that illustrates standard score equivalents.

Exercise #19
STANINES, SAT/ACT, AND GRADE-EQUIVALENT SCORES

This exercise includes a brief article prepared by the Psychological Corporation that explains what stanines are and how they are used. The exercise concludes with three true/false tests challenging the students' interpretive abilities with respect to stanines, SAT/ACT scores, and grade-equivalent scores (see pages 122–124 for the answer keys to these tests).

Exercise #20
NORMS

Students picture themselves as test developers whose task it is to create an exemplary set of norms for a set of class test data.

Exercise #21
THE PEARSON *r*

An explanation of the Pearson *r* is followed by exercises that ask the student to create a scatterplot and from it estimate an answer to a correlational question. Following illustrated step-by-step instructions, the student is walked through the calculation of a Pearson *r* using both the deviation score formula and the raw score formula. It is the student's task to interpret the findings (see page 125 for the answer key to this exercise).

Exercise #22
"HELLO" TO RHO

Rho is introduced along with a step-by-step computational example. Students are also encouraged to convert the data in Exercise #21 to ranks and (a) calculate rho for that data, and (b) compare it to the value obtained for the Pearson *r*. Two additional practice exercises that require the students to calculate rho correlations are provided (see pages 125–126 for the answer key to this exercise).

Exercise #23
OTHER COEFFICIENTS OF CORRELATION

Other coefficients for correlation such as biserial r, the point-biserial r, the tetrachoric r, and the phi coefficient are explained. Given a sample problem, students are asked to calculate and interpret a point-biserial r and a phi coefficient (see pages 126–128 for an answer key to this exercise).

Exercise #24
AN EXERCISE IN REGRESSION

Following an explanation of the concept of regression and a step-by-step illustration of the solution to a regression problem, students are given a sample problem (see pages 128–129 for an answer key to this exercise).

CHAPTER 5

RELIABILITY

Exercise #25
THE CONCEPT OF RELIABILITY

Following a discussion of the concept of reliability, the student is asked to answer three questions "in detail sufficient to exhibit your knowledge of the concept of reliability": (1) Is it possible to develop a test that will be totally free from error variance? Explain why or why not. (2) As an academic exercise, what if you wished to develop an ability-type test that in no way reflected the testtaker's ability? In other words, contrary to the question above where you were asked whether it would be possible to develop a totally error-free test, here you are being asked if it is possible to develop a test that would reflect nothing but error. (3) Describe the role that the concept of *correlation* plays in the concept of *reliability*.

Exercise #26
TEST-RETEST AND INTER-SCORER RELIABILITY

Using sample data, the student in asked to (1) create a scatterplot and estimate test-retest reliability, and (2) calculate and interpret a test-retest reliability coefficient. Another task in this exercise is the calculation and interpretation of rho as a measure of inter-scorer reliability (see pages 130–131 for an answer key to this exercise).

Exercise #27
USING THE SPEARMAN-BROWN FORMULA

Students are asked to apply the Spearman-Brown formula to determine (1) the reliability of a shortened test, and (2) the number of items that would be needed in order to attain a desired level of reliability (see page 131 for an answer key to this exercise).

Exercise #28
UNDERSTANDING INTERNAL CONSISTENCY RELIABILITY

This exercise consists of several tasks, all or some of which you may choose to assign. The tasks the students are assigned include (1) writing a brief essay entitled "The Psychometric Concept of Internal Consistency Reliability"; (2) rewriting this essay after locating and reading three primary sources having to do with methods of obtaining an estimate of internal consistency reliability; (3) describing, in a sentence or two, when each of the three methods of estimating internal consistency reliability (Spearman-Brown formula, coefficient alpha, and KR 20) would be appropriate; and (4) explaining, again in a sentence or two, why a series of three statements are true.

CHAPTER 6
VALIDITY

Exercise #29
THE CONCEPT OF VALIDITY

Following a brief review of the concept of validity, the students are challenged to write a proposal for a grant to conduct a test validation study—or at least a description of how they would go about assessing not only the face validity of a test but its content-, criterion-, and construct-related validity as well.

Exercise #30
THE QUANTIFICATION OF CONTENT VALIDITY

A brief description of the measurement of content validity is followed by some short-answer problems.

Exercise #31
PREDICTING A CRITERION SCORE

A step-by-step illustration of the use of linear regression for prediction with respect to a criterion is followed by a sample problem.

Exercise #32
THE MULTITRAIT-MULTIMETHOD MATRIX

A step-by-step description, with illustrations, of the multitrait-multimethod matrix is presented. Two brief descriptions of research studies including multitrait multimethod matrices are also presented for the student to interpret. Students are then asked to respond to questions based on these matrices that assess their understanding of this method. Sample responses to these questions are provided on pages 132–133.

Exercise #33
FACTOR ANALYSIS AND THE CORRELATION MATRIX

A brief elaboration on the presentation of factor analysis in the text is followed by a task that involves interpretation of a correlation matrix for four items on a true/false test of Introversion/Extroversion. An answer key is provided on page 133.

Exercise #34
FACTOR ANALYSIS AND CONSTRUCT VALIDITY

A construct validity study of 11 measures of impulsivity is described followed by a series of questions that assess the students' understanding of the concept of construct validity and their ability to apply that knowledge. An answer key to this exercise is provided on pages 133–134.

Exercise #35
FAIRNESS AND BIAS

Drawing on their own background and experience, as well as their textbook and a Psychological Corporation article entitled "Fairness and the Matter of Bias," students are asked to describe in their own words (1) a "fair test," (2) a "biased test," and (3) suggestions for eliminating unfair and biased tests.

CHAPTER 7

TEST DEVELOPMENT

Exercise #36
THE TEST DEVELOPMENT PROCESS

Drawing on what they've learned about the test development process from their textbook, as well as a reprinted article entitled "Constructing the Puerto Rico Self-Concept Scale: Problems and Procedures," students are asked to (1) identify the various steps of test development within the article, (2) ask questions about what they would like to know more about with reference to the construction of the discussed scale, and (3) offer suggestions for future directions to the authors of the scale.

Exercise #37
SCALING THE BOUNDS OF CONSCIOUSNESS

Students are asked to read a description of the scaling of a hypothetical Depth of Hypnosis Scale (DHS) and then instructed, drawing upon what they have read in this description and in their text, to write a brief essay on alternative ways the scaling of the DHS could have been approached.

Exercise #38
GUTTMAN SCALING

A sample of an item from a Guttman Scale is presented and the student is then asked to construct his/her own test item using Guttman scaling.

Exercise #39
ITEM ANALYSIS: QUANTITATIVE METHODS

Which items within a pool of possible items represent the best items? Which items need to be modified or eliminated in order to make the test a better test? These are the types of questions that must be quantitatively dealt with in this exercise. Focus is primarily on indices of item difficulty and item discrimination. In preparation for assigning this exercise you may want to have prepared a 10-item list of words representing a broad range of difficulty levels but all appropriate for administration to your class. Make it a well-thought-out list since the results of your spelling test will serve as the raw data for this class exercise in item analysis. An answer key for the items in Part 2 of this exercise is provided on pages 134–135.

Exercise #40
ITEM ANALYSIS: QUALITATIVE METHODS

Two qualitative item analysis methods ("Think Aloud" and "Small Group Discussion") are presented and students are asked to use these techniques to analyze items of the Mid-Pawling Personality Inventory (MPPI, reprinted in Appendix A of 101 Exercises). Variables such as ambiguity, offensiveness, inappropriateness, foolishness, transparency, social desirability, and invasion of privacy are focused on.

Exercise #41
WRITING "GOOD" ITEMS

As an exercise in item writing, students are asked to create their own five-item test on "American History from 1940 to 1980." Additionally, they are to provide a brief rationale for (a) the range of content covered by the test, and (b) the choice of a particular item format. Finally, they must troubleshoot their own items.

CHAPTER 8

INTELLIGENCE AND ITS MEASUREMENT

Exercise #42
THE CONCEPT OF INTELLIGENCE

In stepwise fashion, the student is encouraged to develop his or her own definition of intelligence and then compare it to some existing definitions. This is an important exercise in that it provides a foundation for two exercises to come.

Exercise #43
INTERPRETING IQ SCORES

To help identify possible problem areas with respect to how IQ scores are interpreted, a 10-item true/false test from John R. Hills of Florida State University is presented here (the answer key for this exercise is provided on pages 135–136).

Exercise #44
MENTAL AGE

Students read about the historical concept of mental age and its relationship to IQ. Students are then asked to respond to a series of questions based on their reading.

Exercise #45
SUCCESSIVE AND SIMULTANEOUS PROCESSING

Successive and simultaneous processing are briefly described and two examples giving written directions and a seminar outline of each processing mode are provided. Students are then asked to create two of their own forms of some other stimulus and explain why one is more likely to be processed in successive fashion, while the other is more likely to be processed in simultaneous fashion.

Exercise #46
RATING THE GIFTED

Students are referred back to their text to review an example of a half-dozen items used to rate emotional development of the gifted. Using this rating scale as a model, students are asked to develop a half-dozen items of their own to measure *social* development.

Exercise #47
GRAPPLING WITH SOME MEASUREMENT ISSUES

Building now on not only the conception of intelligence developed by the student but on a test of intelligence devised to measure it, students are confronted with a series of "hard" questions regarding the nature of the test.

Exercise #48
MORE ISSUES, MORE GRAPPLING

The questions raised here are not based on the student's own conception of intelligence but are, among other things, designed to elicit the student's response to the thoughts of others. After being asked to respond to a quote from Shockley and one from Jensen, students are then given an opportunity to voice their own thoughts on issues such as nature versus nurture in intelligence and culture-free versus culture-specific testing.

CHAPTER 9

TESTS OF INTELLIGENCE

Exercise #49
TESTS OF INTELLIGENCE

Building on the previous chapter in which students were asked to develop their own concept of intelligence, this exercise challenges students to outline a fairly detailed plan for a test of intelligence that is consistent with their own conceptualization.

Exercise #50
TAILORING WITHOUT NEEDLES OR THREAD

The concept of adaptive testing is reviewed and instructions on how to create items to be used in this format are provided. The student is given the task of creating three test items, each of a different level of difficulty, to tap a student's knowledge of the material in Chapter 9 of the text. The items must be in a format suitable for an adaptive testing format.

Exercise #51
FACTOR ANALYSIS AND TESTS OF INTELLIGENCE

As an extension of information presented in the Chapter 9 Close-Up, students are asked to conduct an "eyeball" analysis of sample items from the Otis-Lennon School Ability Test (OLSAT). Based on the sample items presented and without conducting a formal factor analysis, students are asked to speculate on the factors they believe the test is measuring. In addition, they are asked to identify the theory that guided the construction of the test from which the sample items were drawn.

Exercise #52
MUCH ADO ABOUT MENSA

The Mensa club for the intellectually gifted is described and sample items from their screening test for membership are presented. Students are asked to write an essay expressing their own thoughts about the organization, as well as the test items used to screen for membership.

Exercise #53
CREATE AN ALTERNATIVE MEASURE OF INTELLECTUAL ABILITY

The student's task in this exercise is to create an alternative measure of intelligence called the "Music Appreciation and Listening Skills (MALS)" test wherein the subject responds to questions after listening to a tape of a popular song. The student then describes (1) a process of norming the test, (2) procedures for determining the test's psychometric soundness, and (3) possible problems foreseen in administering, scoring, and interpreting the test. Additionally, the student is challenged to think about (1) how this test taps some aspect of intelligence not tapped by traditional measures, (2) how this test might be used in everyday practice, (3) how cultural factors might influence scores on this test, and (4) how they might make this test less culture-bound.

Exercise #54
ADMINISTERING THE MALS

Here the student administers the test developed in the previous exercise and troubleshoots problems related to it conceptually, as well as practically (in terms of administration, scoring, and interpretation).

Exercise #55
PICK-A-TEST: TESTS OF INTELLIGENCE

A listing of additional (i.e., beyond what is presented in the text) individual and group tests of intelligence together with a brief description of each is presented. Students are then asked to select one test that they think they would like to know more about. Then, drawing upon all of the resources at their disposal, they respond to a series of seven questions ranging from asking what their chosen test measures to, as a measurement consultant, whether they would recommend this test to clients who are test users, together with a rationale for their recommendation.

CHAPTER 10

PRESCHOOL AND EDUCATIONAL ASSESSMENT

Exercise #56
PRESCHOOL ASSESSMENT: PHYSICAL DEVELOPMENT

The premise in this exercise is that all students in the class will be participating in a presentation at the "Annual Conference of the Experience of Being a Preschool Child." To prepare, three out-of-class exercises in assessment are presented. All three exercises require the cooperation of a parent and a preschooler. It is further recommended that the parent act as the "examiner" in the assessment situation. The first exercise deals with assessing the physical aspects of development including an assessment of motor skills such as walking, skipping, hopping, and catching a ball. Fine motor coordination is assessed by means of "the shoe and sock test" in which the parent asks the child to remove and then put back on his or her shoes and socks.

Exercise #57
PRESCHOOL ASSESSMENT: COGNITIVE DEVELOPMENT

The assessment of the preschooler continues with tasks loosely based on studies of Jean Piaget and others. The child is assessed with respect to tasks involving counting, categorization, and the Piagetian concept of conservation.

Exercise #58
PRESCHOOL ASSESSMENT: LANGUAGE AND SOCIAL DEVELOPMENT

It is recommended that this third and final phase of the assessment of the preschooler be accomplished in a session separate from the first two. Here, the student's task is to observe the preschool child for a two-hour period (including some period of time spent at play with other children) and to prepare a report with reference to specific impressions regarding the child's language and social skills.

Exercise #59
ASSESSMENT IN THE SCHOOLS

The student is asked to play the role of a principal of a private elementary school writing a letter to parents explaining to them the role of psychological tests in their child's education. In writing the letter, students may draw upon not only their textbook and their own background and experience but also four reprinted articles from the Psychological Corporation: "Assessing School Ability," "Selection and Provision of Testing Materials," "Some Things Parents Should Know About Testing," and "On Telling Parents About Test Results."

Exercise #60
STANDARDIZED ACHIEVEMENT TESTS

The task in this exercise is to create a standardized achievement test to evaluate mastery of the material in the text chapter on educational assessment. Students are asked to describe in broad terms how they would go about developing such a standardized achievement test. They are also asked to include a half-dozen or so sample items and a plan for reporting the results to the community. As supplementary material, two informative articles from the Psychological Corporation are reprinted here: "How a Standardized Achievement Test Is Built" and "Reporting Standardized Achievement Test Results in the Community."

Exercise #61
FIRSTHAND PORTFOLIO ASSESSMENT

The concept of a portfolio and the practice of portfolio assessment are reviewed. Students are then given the task of creating their own portfolio to illustrate all they have learned about psychological testing and assessment to date in an effort to convince you they are deserving of an A in your course (despite their exam grades to-date). You are then asked to provide feedback on their portfolio.

Exercise #62
AUTHENTIC ASSESSMENT . . . REALLY!

The concept of authentic assessment is reviewed and students are given the task of creating a way to assess "authentically" a student's knowledge of Chapter 9 (Tests of Intelligence) in their textbook.

Exercise #63
PICK-A-TEST: PRESCHOOL AND EDUCATIONAL MEASURES

Expanding on those presented in Chapter 10 (Preschool and Educational Assessment), a list of preschool and educational tests along with a brief description of each is presented. Students are then asked to select one that they would like to know more about and use all the resources at their disposal to answer a series of questions (identical to those presented in Exercise #55) related to the use of the test, meaning of test scores, and psychometric properties of the test.

CHAPTER 11

PERSONALITY ASSESSMENT: OVERVIEW AND OBJECTIVE METHODS

Exercise #64
"PERSONALITY" AND ITS ASSESSMENT

This exercise parallels some of the previous exercises in the area of intelligence by having students (1) develop their own conception of the meaning of "personality" and (2) develop a relatively detailed plan to measure it. A final question asks which approach to test construction would be used and why.

Exercise #65
GEORGE WASHINGTON'S 16 PF

In an effort to provide the student with firsthand experience with a computerized, narrative report of a widely used personality test, one such report for the scoring and reporting of the 16 PF of George Washington is presented. Yes, it is for George Washington, the "father of our country." The report is based on what several psychologists, familiar with the test and having studied biographical information of George at age 44, think of how he would have scored. Students are then asked to assume the role of a vocational counselor at a large and prestigious counseling firm. Given the file of 44-year-old George Washington, they find this 16 PF report. Based solely on the report, they are asked what type of career they would advise Mr. Washington to pursue and the rationale for that advice including the role of cultural factors in their decision.

Exercise #66
EMPIRICAL-CRITERION KEYING—CALIFORNIA STYLE

A description of the California Personality Inventory (CPI) is presented and the student is asked to complete two tasks: (1) to describe similarities and differences between the CPI and the MMPI-2 and (2) to describe in detail a situation in which a counselor may want to use the CPI with a client and what the objective of the testing would be.

Exercise #67
CLINICAL VERSUS ACTUARIAL PREDICTION

The concepts of actuarial (or statistical) and clinical approaches to assessment are reviewed and implications for personnel selection described. Students are then asked to assume the role of the head of a worldwide corporation, with a workplace characterized as a large multicultural environment, who must hire either Dr. Clin (who employs a clinical approach to making personnel decisions) or Dr. Actu (who uses an actuarial approach) as the head of their personnel department.

Exercise #68
PERSONALITY TEST SCALES

In this exercise, aspects of the structure of personality-test scales are focused on with specific reference to the validity scales of a test such as the MMPI-2. Students are guided to developing their own scales—including a Credibility Scale (CR), an Inconsistency Scale (IN), a Masculinity/Femininity Scale (MF), an Unusual Response Scale (UN-scale), a Faking Scale (FA), as well as another scale of their own creation, for the mock personality test (Mid-Pawling Personality Inventory, MPPI), presented in Appendix A. An answer key for this exercise is presented on pages 136–137.

Exercise #69
"JUST YOUR TYPE"

The personality typology based on body build, proposed by William Sheldon and his associates, is presented. Students are then asked to complete several tasks: (1) the student is asked to choose which body type best describes himself/herself and other people they know; (2) to estimate how accurate they perceive the personality description that characterizes that type, both for themselves and the others they know; (3) to describe the types of validation research that Sheldon and his associates would have to conduct if they wanted to validate his theory, including the types of assessment tools that would be particularly useful and the types of problems likely encountered in this type of research; and (4) to develop their own "Sheldon Scale" for the MPPI consisting of three subscales and at least two MPPI questions each to measure the three body types—endomorphy, ectomorphy, and mesomorphy. An answer key for part 4 of this exercise is provided on pages 137–138.

Exercise #70
PICK-A-TEST: PERSONALITY TESTS

Expanding on the objective methods of personality assessment presented in Chapter 11, a list of personality tests along with a brief description of each is presented. Students are then asked to select one that they would like to know more about and use all the resources at their disposal to answer a series of questions (identical to those presented in earlier Pick-A-Test exercises) related to the use of the test, meaning of test scores, and the psychometric properties of the test.

CHAPTER 12

PROJECTIVE METHODS

Exercise #71
UNDERSTANDING AND USING PROJECTIVE TECHNIQUES

The student's task in this exercise is threefold: to create a projective test battery, administer the battery to a subject, and make an interpretation of the resulting data. The battery will consist of one homemade, monochromatic Rorschach-like inkblot, one TAT-like picture, one word-association test consisting of 10 words, one sentence completion test consisting of 10 stems, and one picture frustration item similar to the items found in the Rosenzweig Picture Frustration Study. You will no doubt wish to supplement the brief guidelines given for administration and interpretation of this test battery.

Exercise #72
THE HOLTZMAN INKBLOT TECHNIQUE

A description and discussion of the psychometric properties of the Holtzman Inkbot Technique (HIT) are presented. Students are then asked to assume the role of an invited speaker at the centennial meeting of "The International Rorschach Society" giving a talk on "A Call for More Research on the HIT." Students then write a five-minute speech designed to compel the society members to devote more time to exploiting the full potential of the Holtzman Inkblot Technique.

Exercise #73
THE SZONDI TEST

An oddity in the history of psychological testing, and more specifically in the area of projective assessment, the Szondi Test is described. Students are then asked to imagine a turn-of-the-century (i.e., twenty-first century) debate between Lipot Szondi and a member of the editorial board for *Psychometrica*. Students are then instructed to write position statements for both parties.

Exercise #74
THE PSYCHOMETRIC SOUNDNESS OF PROJECTIVE METHODS

Students play the role of a consultant to the creator of a new inkblot test who would like advice on how to go about establishing the reliability and validity of her test. The problems inherent in conducting such research and some suggestions for how the test developer might proceed should be a part of the student's advice.

Exercise #75
PICK-A-TEST: PROJECTIVE PERSONALITY MEASURES

Expanding on the projective methods of personality assessment presented in Chapter 12, a list of projective personality tests along with a brief description of each is presented. Students are then asked to select one that they would like to know more about and use all the resources at their disposal to answer a series of questions (identical to those presented in earlier Pick-A-Test exercises) related to the use of the test, the meaning of test scores, and the psychometric properties of the test.

CHAPTER 13

OTHER PERSONALITY AND BEHAVIORAL MEASURES

Exercise #76
THE Q-SORT AND THE CONCEPT OF SELF

Following a review of what a Q-sort is and how it is used, the student is asked to (1) create a Q-sort by writing 10 trait terms on 10 index cards, one to a card; (2) sort the cards according to "how you see yourself today"; (3) sort the cards again according to "how you would ideally like to be"; and (4) write an interpretation of the findings that includes an explanation for any observed self/ideal self discrepancy and an action plan for reducing those discrepancies over the course of the next few years.

This exercise would appear to be an excellent bridge to the subject matter of Chapter 14, Clinical and Counseling Assessment.

Exercise #77
SITUATIONAL PERFORMANCE MEASURES

The class is broken up into small groups, three or four students to a group, in order to role-play a real-life situational performance measure—a road test for a driver's license. While the driving student must perform three simple maneuvers (one left turn, one right turn, and parallel parking) while being evaluated by the riders, each of the riders must be a full-time behavioral observer and rater. Appropriate cautions are provided though you may want to emphasize them again yourself. In case of inclement weather or other prevailing conditions the day you have planned to assign this task, another situational performance measure—such as a typing test—could be substituted.

Exercise #78
BEHAVIORAL OBSERVATION

In order to obtain firsthand experience in behavioral assessment, students are asked to devise and then use a behavioral observation task designed to assess some aspect of an individual's social skills. Students then role-play an interaction of seeking a self-introduction to someone the assessee is attracted to at a cocktail party and the assessor provides constructive feedback based on their behavioral assessment.

Exercise #79
PICK-A-TEST: MEASURES OF SPECIFIC ASPECTS OF PERSONALITY

Expanding on the measures of personality presented in Chapter 13, a list of personality tests focused on a particular aspect of personality along with a brief description of each is presented. Students are then asked to select one that they would like to know more about and use all the resources at their disposal to answer a series of questions (identical to those presented in earlier Pick-A-Test exercises) related to the use of the test, the meaning of test scores, and the psychometric properties of the test.

CHAPTER 14

CLINICAL AND COUNSELING ASSESSMENT

Exercise #80
THE INTERVIEW AS A TOOL OF ASSESSMENT

One student comes to the head of the class to role-play "a depressed oil heir/heiress" while another role-plays a clinician/interviewer conducting a by-the-book mental status interview (see textbook for details). The rest of the class is the attentive, note-taking audience as the interviewer probes for signs and symptoms of depression. A listing of such signs and symptoms supplements the material in this exercise. Just prior to terminating the interview, questions from the floor are entertained. As the interview is concluded, all students retire to write their own reports describing the mental status of the depressed interviewee.

Exercise #81
THE CASE STUDY

Students read a somewhat controversial (but highly intriguing) case study ("Socially Reinforced Obsessing: Etiology of a Disorder of a Christian Scientist") and after reading Harris (1979) are asked to distinguish between different types of statements made in the case study.

Exercise #82
BEHAVIORAL OBSERVATION

The exercise entails a brief field trip to the school cafeteria for the purpose of some behavioral observation. Students select one visibly overweight individual and one visibly underweight individual and unobtrusively observe not only what is on their lunch trays but exactly how it is consumed as well (for example, who, if anyone, eats faster?). A brief report describing what was observed and any implications stemming from the observations concludes the exercise.

Exercise #83
P. T. BARNUM AND THE MPPI

As part of Exercise #16 and again in Exercise #71 students administered personality tests to a subject. As part of the present exercise, this subject is given feedback on his or her testing of the variety used in studies of the Barnum effect. Is the effect shown in a number of studies replicated? How do subjects rate the bogus feedback they receive? All students report back to the class to share their experience. And by the way, all subjects must not only be thanked—and perhaps taken to lunch—but properly debriefed as well.

Exercise #84
THE MULTITRAIT-MULTIMETHOD MATRIX REVISITED

A multitrait-multimethod matrix drawn from a construct validity study of the MCMI-II is presented. Students are asked to study the tables and respond to a series of questions about the data presented. An answer key for this exercise is provided on page 138.

Exercise #85
PICK-A-TEST: CLINICAL MEASURES

Expanding on the clinical measures presented in Chapter 14, a list of other clinical measures along with a brief description of each is presented. Students are then asked to select one that they would like to know more about and use all the resources at their disposal to answer a series of questions (identical to those presented in earlier Pick-A-Test exercises) related to the use of the test, the meaning of test scores, and the psychometric properties of the test.

CHAPTER 15

NEUROPSYCHOLOGICAL ASSESSMENT

Exercise #86
THE NEUROPSYCHOLOGICAL EXAMINATION

Students pair off and play the role of a neuropsychologist performing a routine neuropsychological examination (though they have only a few neuropsychological tests from which to choose for administration). At the conclusion of the examination, the examining "doctor" writes a report on the findings.

Exercise #87
INTERVIEW WITH A NEUROPSYCHOLGOIST

The student's task here is to create a 10-item interview with a neuropsychologist and then conduct the interview. Where there is an abundance of such personnel available in the area, students may be left to their own resources in terms of arranging such interviews. However, if there is a shortage of such personnel available in your area for such an exercise, it will be more feasible to invite a neuropsychologist to class and have some of the students administer their interviews to the guest in the class setting.

Exercise #88
PICK-A-TEST: NEUROPSYCHOLOGICAL TESTS

Expanding on the neuropsychological tests presented in Chapter 15, a list of other neuropsychological tests along with a brief description of each is presented. Students are then asked to select one that they would like to know more about and use all the resources at their disposal to answer a series of questions (identical to those presented in earlier Pick-A-Test exercises) related to the use of the test, the meaning of test scores, and the psychometric properties of the test.

CHAPTER 16

THE ASSESSMENT OF PEOPLE WITH DISABLING CONDITIONS

Exercise #89
ADMINISTERING, SCORING, AND INTERPRETING NONSTANDARDIZED PSYCHOLOGICAL TESTS

This exercise is designed to enhance the students' appreciation of the problems inherent in administering and interpreting psychological tests to people with disabling conditions when (1) adaptations must be made in the test in order to administer it, and (2) interpretation of the test results must be made despite the fact that a nonstandardized test administration took place. Generalizing from the descriptions of various Wechsler subtests, the student, in the role of the school district advisor, is challenged to adapt each of the subtests for administration to a testtaker who is either vision- or hearing-impaired. It is also the student advisor's difficult task to suggest guidelines for scoring and interpreting the test protocols.

Exercise #90
ASSESSING ADAPTIVE BEHAVIOR

Students are presented with a list of the general areas from which items found in a test of adaptive behavior may be drawn. The task in this exercise is to (1) create one item to measure behavior from each of the general areas listed, and (2) administer this homemade test to anyone who will sit for it. Students are then asked to discuss the problems and pitfalls in (a) devising such a test, (b) administering such a test, (c) scoring such a test, and (d) interpreting the findings.

Exercise #91
PICK-A-TEST: THE ASSESSMENT OF PEOPLE WITH DISABLING CONDITIONS

Expanding on the tests used for persons with disabling conditions presented in Chapter 16, a list of other such tests along with a brief description of each is presented. Students are then asked to select one that they would like to know more about and use all the resources at their disposal to answer a series of questions (identical to those presented in earlier Pick-A-Test exercises) related to the use of the test, the meaning of test scores, and the psychometric properties of the test.

CHAPTER 17

INDUSTRIAL/ORGANIZATIONAL ASSESSMENT

Exercise #92
ASSESSMENT OF PERSONNEL

A brief review of terms such as "screening," "selection," "classification," and "placement" is followed by an exercise wherein students are asked to picture themselves as NASA personnel psychologists. What types of tests or measurement procedures would they use for the purpose of screening applicants for a manned mission? What types of tests or measurement procedures would they use for the purpose of selecting applicants? Beyond the written exercise, an in-class employment interview with role-playing students may be enlightening.

Exercise #93
TEST PROFILES

A review of the nature and use of profiles in intelligence testing and personality testing as well as personnel testing is followed by data on a hypothetical aptitude test. The student's task is to (1) graph the data in both frequency polygon and histogram form, (2) provide vocational advice to the testtaker, and (3) create an aptitude test profile for an individual who might be ideally suited to enter the field of psychology and specialize in the area of psychometrics.

Exercise #94
ANOTHER DAY, ANOTHER PROFILE

Students are introduced to the Differential Aptitude Test (DAT) and then asked to (1) predict how John D. Doe, introduced in Exercise #93, would perform on each of the eight subtests of the DAT; (2) how an individual ideally suited for the specialty of psychometrics would score on the DAT subtests, and (3) to write a short argument, taking either a pro or con position, regarding the substitution of the DAT for a measure of intelligence in a research study.

Exercise #95
YOUR PERSONALITY SUITS YOU FOR WORK AS . . .

Students are introduced to the Guilford-Zimmerman Temperament Survey (GZTS). They are then asked to (1) create their own GZTS profile by characterizing themselves as either "low," "medium," or "high" with regard to each of the 10 GZTS dimensions described in the exercise; (2) describe what type of work they think they are best suited for, based on their profile; and (3) create one question that can be answered in a yes/no format to measure each of the 10 dimensions of the GZTS followed by a discussion of their perceptions of the ease or difficulty of this task including the obstacles that must be overcome when creating such questions.

Exercise #96
PICK-A-TEST: INDUSTRIAL/ORGANIZATIONAL ASSESSMENT

Expanding on the tests used for industrial/organizational assessment presented in Chapter 17, a list of other such tests along with a brief description of each is presented. Students are then asked to select one that they would like to know more about and use all the resources at their disposal to answer a series of questions (identical to those presented in earlier Pick-A-Test exercises) related to the use of the test, the meaning of test scores, and the psychometric properties of the test.

CHAPTER 18

CONSUMER ASSESSMENT

Exercise #97
TASTE TESTS

We have all been exposed to advertising that boasts superiority on the basis of taste preference or discrimination data. Such research, as presented in most advertising, seem deceptively simple. The purpose of this exercise is to sensitize students to some of the issues involved in such experimentation. Students are encouraged to design and execute a taste test between two brands of carbonated drinks. The test—however designed—is conducted with 10 people the student knows (or can persuade to participate). After a report of the findings is written, students consult references in the professional literature (such as those at the end of Chapter 18) to see if there are any issues in taste-discrimination testing that they have overlooked. They then make a list of these overlooked issues and come prepared to discuss them in class. Their second task, related to using in-depth interviewing in consumer assessment, is to gain experience in actually conducting in-depth interviews by devising a list of questions to "get at the heart" of why people they know are loyal to different brands of beer. They are asked to identify at least six different people who are loyal to three different beers and administer their interview to these individuals. They then write a brief report of their findings.

Exercise #98
PSYCHOGRAPHICS

In an effort to acquaint students with the consumer psychology system of psychographics and the place of measurement and categorization within that system, students are provided with background information on demography and its application in marketing referred to as psychographics. Students are then asked to assume the role of a consumer psychologist and respond to three scenarios (a carmaker who has developed "the mother of all luxury cars," a clothing manufacturer who is interested in marketing a new fabric, and a dairy products distributor who has developed a new food) with reference to the Stanford Research Institute's VALS (Values and Life Style) taxonomy.

CHAPTER 19

COMPUTER-ASSISTED PSYCHOLOGICAL ASSESSMENT

Exercise #99
COMPUTER-ASSISTED PSYCHOLOGICAL ASSESSMENT

In the role of a computer-savvy psychologist consultant, the student is asked to speak before the "Traditional Clinicians Club" on the pros, cons, and issues attendant to computerizing a clinical practice. The class plays the "club" as individual students present their five-minute talks followed by an equally brief question/answer session.

Exercise #100
COMPUTER-ASSISTED EDUCATIONAL ASSESSSMENT: THE CASE OF THE GRE

Background information, including advantages and disadvantages, of the computerized version of the Graduate Record Examination (GRE) as compared to the paper-and-pencil version is presented. Students are then asked to respond to three questions from the perspective of a testtaker.

Exercise #101
PICK-A-TEST: COMPUTER-ASSISTED TEST PRODUCTS

Expanding on the discussion of computer-assisted test products presented in Chapter 19, a list of other such products, along with a brief description of each, is presented. Students are then asked to select one that they would like to know more about and use all the resources at their disposal to answer a series of questions (identical to those presented in earlier Pick-A-Test exercises) related to the use of the test/product, meaning of the test scores provided, and the psychometric properties of the test/product. If a traditional (paper-and-pencil) version of the test exists, students are also asked to respond as to whether they would or would not prefer to administer the computerized version.

Part 2
Answers to Selected Exercises

Exercise #17
Transformed Scores: Percentiles

Exercise #19
Stanines, SAT/ACT, and Grade-Equivalent Scores

The answers to each of the 10-item true/false tests contained in Exercises #17 and #19 are provided by Professor John R. Hills of Florida State University.[1]

Answers to Test on Percentile Scores

Question 8 is true. The others are false.

Explanations:

1. Percentile scores indicate the relative standing in a group, not the percentage of items that are correct.

2. Mary's score is a number correct score. One cannot tell whether this is a good score without knowing the performances of others or having a carefully justified cutoff score which reflects mastery. In fact, one cannot be sure that Tim's score, which was a percentile, reflects better-than-average reading without at least knowing the norm group from which his percentile score is obtained.

3. Scores of the 30th percentile are really not far below average. Usually no more than a few percent of a class are failed, say 3 or 4 percent, not anywhere near 30 percent. Besides, a nationally standardized test may not accurately sample the arithmetic skills covered in Susie's class.

4. An increase of 9 percentile units at the top or bottom of the scale represents an improvement of many more items than the same increase near the middle of the scale. On that basis, one could conclude that Bill made much more progress than Jim.

5. Rebecca's score is one standard deviation above the mean. Sally's score is two standard deviations above the mean, and Jeanne's score is three standard deviations above the mean. In terms of score scales such as standard scores, which more accurately reflect the distribution of test scores and differences between them, these students are equally far apart in achievement. The percentile scale distorts the distances between scores.

6. The 50th percentile is near the center of the distribution. If it is to be near the center, some scores must be below it and some above. It is unrealistic to try to get everyone up to the center. If everyone does improve, or if only the bottom half improve, the median (50th percentile) also increases. While the change in median will not appear on the form of the test now being used, the next time the test is standardized, the median will move up if enough of the students below the median nationally show substantial improvement.

7. The average of percentile ranks is not itself a percentile rank. To get percentile ranks for averages of percentile ranks, one would have to rank the average percentile ranks and get a new set of percentiles for these average ranks.

---

[1]Reprinted with permission from *Hills' Handy Hints* published by the National Council on Measurement in Education (1986).

8. The scores for a class cannot be averaged to evaluate the average score in terms of the norms table for scores of individuals. Class averages can only be evaluated in terms of a norms table for class averages. Some publishers do not provide norms for class averages. In such cases, a comparison between the average score of a class and the average scores of other classes cannot sensibly be made. The spread of class averages is much less than the spread of individual scores.

9. When one considers the standard error of measurement for scores such as those of Rebecca and Helmut, it is possible that those scores could be reversed in position on another testing. The percentile band concept is used to keep from overinterpreting small differences between scores.

10. On most tests the percentile bands near the middle of the score distribution are wide. That signifies that we do not know precisely what a student like Gretchen's reading level really is. Obtaining the percentile rank of her score instead of the percentile band gives the appearance of greater accuracy, but this is only an illusion. There is no practical way to obtain Gretchen's true score, of course.

Answers to Test on Stanine Scores

Explanations:

1. No. Stanine scores are numbers from 1 to 9. There is no such thing as a stanine score of zero. A zero score reported as a stanine indicates that an error has been made.

2. Yes and no. Stanine 5 is in the middle of the scale, and in that sense Bill got an average score on the test. However, each stanine represents a band of scores, not a specific score. The 5th stanine extends from the 40th to the 60th percentile. So Bill might be performing as low as the 40th percentile or as high as the 60th percentile but still receive a stanine of 5. However, because the stanine scale reflects a normal curve, the 40th percentile is usually only a few raw score points lower than the 60th percentile.

3. No. Stanines are represented by the single-digit whole numbers, such as 1, 2, and 3, never by numbers with decimal points. Except for the first and ninth stanines, each stanine represents a narrow band of scores on the test. (The first and ninth stanines may be very wide in terms of raw score points. Each extends to the beginning or end of the test, however far that may be.) Thus, a stanine of 6.5 does not exist. Anyone who uses such a number for a stanine has made an error.

4. No. The ninth stanine is not the 96th percentile. The lower limit of the ninth stanine is the 96th percentile, but the upper limit is plus infinity. Any performance above the 96th percentile is the 9th stanine. Cindy may have scored far above the 96th percentile and received a stanine of 9. The same is true at the other end of the scale for a stanine of 1. A person with a stanine score of 1 may be as high as the 4th percentile, or very much lower.

5. Yes. Three easy landmarks for relating stanines to standard scores are the mean and plus and minus one standard deviation. The mean is in the middle of the fifth stanine. Plus one standard deviation is in the middle of the seventh stanine. Minus one standard deviation is in the middle of the third stanine.

6. Yes. Ms. Billingsley used the *Rule for Four*. With stanines, a close approximation to the distribution of scores can be remembered as starting with 4 percent in either stanine 1 or 9, then adding 4 percent for the next stanine each time up to stanine 5 and then subtracting 4 percent for each to the end of the scale. Thus, the percent of the scores that are assigned 1, 2, 3, . . . 9 are very close to 4, 8, 12, 16, 20, 16, 12, 8, and 4, respectively. So Ms. Billingsley said to herself, "Four percent for stanine 9, 8 percent for stanine 8, and 12 percent for stanine 7." Then she had her answer. She could have started with stanine 5, saying to herself, "Twenty percent in stanine 5, 16 percent in stanine 6, and 12 percent in stanine 7," reaching the same result.

7. No. First, to be correct a decile is a point, not a range. The first decile is the score that separates the lowest scoring 10 percent of scores from the highest scoring 90 percent, for example. The name for the lowest 10 percent is the lowest *tenth*, or the first *tenth*, not the first *decile*. Beyond that, the first tenth is the lowest scoring 10 percent, but the first stanine is the lowest scoring 4 percent, a much lower scoring group, on the average. In general, the only correspondence between tenths of a distribution (or "deciles") and stanines is that tenths and stanines above 5 are high scoring and below 5 are low scoring. The differences between tenths and stanines reflect different assumptions about the distribution of scores. Tenths are based on the assumption that scores have a rectangular or flat distribution. Stanines are based on the more realistic assumption that scores are distributed normally.

8. No. Tests that use stanine scores refer these scores to students in a particular grade, not to students in general or to people in general. So a student who regularly receives stanine scores of 5 in a subject from year to year can be assumed to be making normal progress. He stays in the middle of the distribution. Another student who continually makes scores of stanine 7 stays about 1 standard deviation above the mean and makes normal progress also. Normal progress with stanines (or with percentiles or standard scores) is shown by earning the same score over time, not higher scores year by year.

9. No. Mr. Tatnall does not need to worry much about a change from one stanine score to the adjacent stanine score. One correct question fewer could move a person one stanine down if his score was at the bottom of the range for that stanine. This is one of the problems with stanine scores. A person's performance can be anywhere in a range of scores but receive the same stanine. If Patricia scored at the lower edge of the fifth stanine, a trivial difference in performance could change her score to the next lower stanine.

10. Yes. When scores differ by two stanines, we tend to think of there being a real difference, not an error of measurement. Other things being equal, for tests with satisfactory reliabilities (.90), such differences are expected to occur only about one time in ten. Therefore, differences that large deserve further investigation. Perhaps Elena has benefitted from some effective teaching, or she may have become more motivated, or she may have found more time to read, or something in her life that was impeding her progress may have been removed. A difference that large is unlikely to be an accident.

Answers to Test on SAT and ACT Scores

Answers:

1. N, 2. N, 3. N, 4. N, 5. N, 6. Y, 7. N, 8. Y, 9. N, 10. N

Explanations:

1. The "average" SAT score depends on whose data are being averaged. The score 500 was the average of 10,654 students who took the SAT in April of 1941. Since then, a process called equating has been used to ensure that the aptitude level represented by 500 in April 1941 is the same level represented by a score of 500 on a SAT taken at any other time. However, in 1983, the mean scores of all college-bound seniors tested were 430 on Verbal and 420 on Mathematics, for boys, and 493 and 445, respectively, for girls. The means for all high school seniors would, of course, be appreciably lower. We know now that mean SAT scores fluctuate from year to year, and until recently they have been declining. The score 500 is probably not the mean for any existing naturally constituted group.

2. Mary must have added together her SAT-V and SAT-M scores to get 900. The highest reported score for either test is 800, so 900 cannot be a score from either section by itself. Susie's scores added together are 900, the same as Mary's scores. The College Board does not advocate adding V and M scores together for any purpose. In fact, if they are to be combined for estimating future success in college, experience indicates that a better general-purpose combination would be 2V + M, with a minimum of 600 and a maximum of 2400.

Answers to Test on Grade-Equivalent Scores

Question 1 is true. The others are false.

Explanations:

1. Because GE scores are developed by obtaining the mean or median performance at each of several grade levels on a test whose content covers the several grades, a student who scores above the grade in which he is enrolled has performed above average for students in his grade.

2. A student can obtain a GE score without being able to do the work of students at the grade level indicated by his score. Tim may have obtained a 9.2 score by getting *all* the items that were designed for grades 4, 5, 6, and 7 correct and may not have done particularly well on items designed for grades 8 and 9, if there were any.

3. Often the GEs associated with high or low number-correct scores are obtained by extrapolation. It is possible that no ninth grader was ever tested with the test given Tim.

4. Because Tim could have gotten a GE score of 9.2 by doing well on the easier or lower-level items of the test, one cannot tell from these scores whether he could participate effectively with ninth graders or not.

5. In most schools, reading is not taught in the ninth grade except perhaps for remediation of ineffective reading skills. So it does not make sense to consider putting Tim into ninth grade instruction in reading. Even if reading (or any subject for which a 9.2 GE was obtained) were taught at the ninth grade, one would not know whether Tim should be put into a higher level of instruction without evaluating whether he had the prerequisite skills. The GE score cannot be relied on to indicate that ninth grade skills have been mastered.

6. The standard deviations of GE scores vary from one subject to another. Tim's score of 9.2 on reading and 7.3 on arithmetic could be equal scores if one used another score scale such as percentiles. The difference between the two GE scores may be due to the fact that students tend to differ less within a grade on arithmetic than on reading. In addition, GE scores above a student's grade do not mean that he has really mastered skills beyond his own grade level.

7. Because the standard deviations for different subjects differ, we cannot tell whether 9.2 in reading is relatively better than 7.3 in arithmetic, and neither necessarily implies that Tim is ahead of his own class.

8. When GE scores have been extrapolated far above or below a student's grade level, it often occurs that even a single additional item correct can change a student's GE score by more than a year. Tim may simply have gotten one or two fewer items correct in the spring than in the fall.

9. The GE score is based on a mean. One dare not expect all students to be at our above grade level on GE scores. In a typical heterogeneous class, about half would obtain GE scores below grade level and half above grade level. Because only 30 percent of Mr. Brown's fifth graders got GE scores below 5.0, his students may be doing a little better than usual instead of worse.

10. Another peculiar characteristic of GE scores is that the standard deviations get larger year by year. Suppose that a person (or a group average) is at and remains at a given percentile score, say the 16th percentile (which is one standard deviation below the mean). This same percentile each year is translated into a lower GE each year because the standard deviation gets larger from year to year. This can leave the impression that a person (or group) is falling farther behind each year. Similarly, if a student (or group average) is above the mean and stays at that same relative position, he appears to get farther ahead every year in terms of GE scores. This is an illusion created by the GE score system.

Exercise #21
The Pearson r

Final examination data for 10 students of the "Home Study School of Elvis Presley Impersonators" are presented along with a record of the actual number of hours each student spent preparing for the examination. Students are asked to (1) create a scatterplot to represent these data, and (2) calculate the Pearson product-moment correlation coefficient (having been provided with formulas, and step-by-step instructions on how to do so). The correct calculations for both the raw score and deviation score Pearson r formulas are presented below.

Calculation of the Pearson r

Raw Data		Deviation Formula Calculations					Raw Score Formula Calculations		
X	Y	$x = X - \bar{X}$	$y = Y - \bar{Y}$	xy	x^2	y^2	XY	X^2	Y^2
23.0	98.0	12.1	22.3	269.83	146.41	497.29	2254	529	9604
16.9	92.0	5.1	16.3	73.13	26.91	265.69	1472	256	8464
.5	45.0	−10.4	−30.7	319.28	108.16	942.49	22.5	.25	2025
12.0	80.0	1.1	4.3	4.73	1.21	18.49	960	144	6400
9.0	76.0	−1.9	.3	−.57	3.61	.09	684	81	5776
10.0	57.0	−.9	−18.7	16.83	.81	349.69	570	100	3249
1.0	61.0	−9.9	−14.7	145.53	98.01	216.09	61	1	3721
14.0	88.0	3.1	12.3	38.13	9.61	151.29	1232	.196	7744
8.5	70.0	−2.4	−5.7	13.68	5.76	32.49	595	72.25	4900
15.0	90.0	4.1	14.3	58.63	16.81	204.49	1350	225	8100

Exercise #22
"Hello" to Rho

As an introduction to some facility in calculating Spearman's rho (and subsequently other correlation coefficients) students are presented with a scenario involving 10 beauty school students and the following variables: (1) sex, (2) score on a pre-test, (3) score on a post-test, and (4) career disposition. Students are instructed to calculate rho and are asked:

> Is there a relationship between the pre-admission score on the qualifying examination and the comprehensive end-of-course examination? If so, how would you describe it?

Having calculated rho for the beauty school problem, the student is then asked to return to the Presley Course data (used earlier to calculate a Pearson r) and calculate rho for it. The computations used to calculate rho in each of these cases follow below.

Note in the beauty school problem that rank order of "A" scores proceeded with a rank of 1 being assigned to the score of 91 (the highest score), a rank of 2 being assigned to 88 (the next-highest score), and so forth. The lowest score in the distribution (64) was assigned a rank of 10. The "A" score of 79 had a frequency of two and was assigned a rank of 6.5. And since each score of 79 was assigned a rank of 6.5, the next lower score is assigned a rank of 8.

Calculation of Spearman's Rho for the Rankings by Professors Go and Nogo

Student	Professor Go's Rankings	Professor Nogo's Rankings	d	d^2
Tiffany	5	3	2	4
Levelor	1	2	−1	1
Harley	4	4	0	0
Macy	9	7	2	4
Dreyfus	8	8	0	0
Scotch	2	1	1	1
Andersen	10	9	1	1
Visine	7	10	−3	9
Hershey	3	6	−3	9
Chrysler	6	5	1	1

$$r_S = 1 - \frac{6Sd^2}{n^3 - n} = 1 - \frac{6(30)}{10^3 - 10} = 1 - \frac{180}{990}$$

$$r_S = 1 - .1818 = .8182$$

Calculation of Spearman's Rho for the Reading Rank-Order Test

Student	First Administration	Second Administration	d	d^2
Kimba	1	3	−2	4
Julep	2	1	1	1
Steve	3	2	1	1
Edie	4	6	−2	4
Nodu	5	7	−2	4
Ike	6	5	1	1
Tina	7	4	3	9

$$r_S = 1 - \frac{6Sd^2}{n^3 - n} = 1 - \frac{6(24)}{7^3 - 7} = 1 - \frac{144}{336}$$

$$r_S = 1 - .4286 = .5714$$

Exercise #23
Other Coefficients of Correlation

Using the beauty school data, students are asked to calculate the coefficient of correlation that expresses the relationship between score on the entry-level test, and sex. Since one variable is continuous in nature and the other is a true dichotomy, the appropriate statistic for the calculation of a correlation coefficient is the point-biserial r. The calculations for the computation of r_{pb} are shown below.

Point Biserial Coefficient of Correlation Problem

Sex of Subject	Score on Entry Level Test	Calculations $(X - \bar{X}^2)$
Male = 0	86	$(86 - 79.7)^2 = 39.69$
Female = 1	91	$(91 - 79.7)^2 = 127.69$
Male = 0	75	$(75 - 79.7)^2 = 22.09$
Female = 1	64	$(64 - 79.7)^2 = 246.49$
Female = 1	73	$(73 - 79.7)^2 = 44.89$
Male = 0	82	$(82 - 79.7)^2 = 5.29$
Male = 0	79	$(79 - 79.7)^2 = .49$
Female = 1	79	$(79 - 79.7)^2 = .49$
Male = 0	88	$(88 - 79.7)^2 = 68.89$
Female = 1	80	$(80 - 79.7)^2 = .09$

Calculating a Point-Biserial r

$$\bar{X}_1 = \frac{SX_1}{n_1} = \frac{91 + 64 + 73 + 79 + 80}{5} = \frac{387}{5} = 77.4$$

$$\bar{X}_0 = \frac{SX_0}{n_0} = \frac{86 + 75 + 82 + 79 + 88}{5} = \frac{410}{5} = 82$$

$$\bar{X} = SX_0 + SX_1 = \frac{387 + 410}{10} = \frac{797}{10} = 79.7$$

$$r_{pb} = \sqrt{n_1 n_0} \left(\frac{\bar{X}_1 - \bar{X}_0}{\sqrt{S(X - \bar{X}^2)}} \right) = \sqrt{\frac{(5)(5)}{10}} \left(\frac{77.4 - 82}{556.1} \right)$$

$$r_{pb} = 1.58(-.195) @ -.3081$$

The phi coefficient is a coefficient of correlation appropriate for use with two true dichotomies. Again with reference to the beauty school example, the student is asked to calculate the relationship between the variables of occupational entry into the field of beauty (represented in the computations below as X), and sex (represented in the computations below as Y). A 0/1 coding system has also been employed in the present example for both occupational disposition (where 0 = did not enter field of beauty, and 1 = did enter field of beauty) and sex (where 0 = male, and 1 = female).

Calculating a Phi Coefficient

		(X) Entered Beauty Field?		
		No (0)	Yes (1)	Total
(Y) Sex	Male (0)	3	2	5
	Female (1)	2	3	5
Total		5	5	10

$$\varphi_{XY} = \frac{p_{(XY)1} - (p_{X1})(p_{Y1})}{\sqrt{(p_{X1})(p_{Y1})(1 - p_{X1})(1 - p_{Y1})}}$$

$$\varphi_{XY} = \frac{.30 - (.5)(.5)}{\sqrt{(.5)(1 - .5)(.5)(1 - .5)}} = \frac{.30 - .25}{\sqrt{(.25)(.25)}}$$

$$= \frac{.05}{\sqrt{.0625}} = \frac{.05}{.25} = .2$$

$$\varphi_{XY} = .2$$

A further word of explanation about the calculations above:

$p_{(XY)1}$ is the proportion of subjects "scoring" 1 on both X and Y; it is equal to 3/10, or .30.

p_{X1} is the proportion of subjects "scoring" 1 on X; it is equal to 5/10, or .5.

p_{Y1} is the proportion of subjects "scoring" 1 on Y; it is equal to 5/10, or .5.

Exercise #24
An Exercise in Regression

The calculations are as follows:

X	Y	XY	X^2	Y^2
10	10	100	100	100
30	20	600	900	400
50	30	1500	2500	900
60	40	2400	3600	1600
70	50	3500	4900	2500
80	60	4800	6400	3600

$$n = 6$$
$$SXY = 12{,}900$$
$$SXSY = 63{,}000$$
$$(SX)^2 = 90{,}000$$
$$SX^2 = 18{,}400$$

Calculations for the Least-Squares Line

$$SX = 300 \qquad\qquad SXY = 12900$$

$$(SX)^2 = (300)^2 = 90000 \qquad\qquad (SX)(SY) = (300)(210)$$

$$SX^2 = 18400 \qquad\qquad\qquad\qquad = 63000$$

$$\bar{X} = \frac{SX}{N} = \frac{300}{6} = 50 \qquad\qquad \bar{Y} = \frac{SY}{N} = \frac{210}{6} = 35$$

$$\hat{y} = a + bX$$

$$b = \frac{SXY - N\bar{X}\bar{Y}}{SX^2 - N\bar{X}^2} = \frac{12900 - 6(50)(35)}{18400 - 6(50)^2}$$

$$b = \frac{12900 - 10500}{18400 - 6(2500)} = \frac{2400}{18400 - 15000} = \frac{2400}{3400} = .70588$$

$$a = \bar{Y} - b\bar{X}$$

$$a = 35 - .70588(50)$$

$$a = 35 - 35.294$$

$$a = -.294$$

Thus, $\hat{y} = -.294 + .70588X$, and for each unit increase in X, the predicted value for Y would increase by .70588X.

$$\hat{y} = -.294 + .70588X, \text{ if } X = 78, \text{ the estimated score } \hat{y} \text{ would be equal to,}$$

$$\hat{y} = -.294 + .70588(78)$$

$$\hat{y} = -.294 + 55.05864$$

$$\hat{y} = 54.76$$

Exercise #26
Test-Retest and Inter-scorer Reliability

Here students are asked to calculate coefficients of test-retest and inter-scorer reliability, using respectively the Pearson r and Spearman's rho. The data and the calculations are as follows:

| Student | X | Y | Pearson r | | | Spearman Rank Order | | | |
			XY	X^2	Y^2	R(X)	R(Y)	d	d^2
Malcolm	98	84	8232	9604	7056	1	6	–5	25
Heywood	92	97	8924	8464	9409	2	2	0	0
Mervin	45	63	2835	2025	3969	10	10	0	0
Zeke	80	91	7280	6400	8281	5	4	1	1
Sam	76	87	6612	5776	7569	6	5	1	1
Macy	57	92	5244	3249	8464	9	3	6	36
Elvis 2	61	98	5978	3721	9604	8	1	7	49
Jed	88	69	6072	7744	4761	4	9	–5	25
Jeb70	70	4900	4900	4900	7	8	–1	1
Leroy	90	75	6750	8100	5625	3	7	–4	16

Calculations for Pearson r

$$SX = 757$$

$$(SX)^2 = (757)^2 = 573049$$

$$SX^2 = 59983$$

$$SY = 826$$

$$(SY)^2 = (826)^2 = 682276$$

$$SY^2 = 69638$$

$$SXY = 62827$$

$$(SX)(SY) = (757)(826) = 625282$$

$$r = \frac{NSXY - SXSY}{\sqrt{[NSX^2 - (SX)^2][NSY^2 - (SY)^2]}}$$

$$r = \frac{10(62827) - 625282}{\sqrt{[10(59983) - 573049][10(69638) - 682276]}}$$

$$r = \frac{2988}{\sqrt{[26781][14104]}} = \frac{2988}{19435} = .1537$$

Calculations for Spearman Rank Order Correlation Coefficient
rho r_s

$$r_S = 1 - \frac{6Sd^2}{N^3 - N}$$

$$r_S = 1 - \frac{6(154)}{10^3 - 10}$$

$$r_S = 1 - \frac{924}{990}$$

$$r_S = 1 - .933$$

$$r_S = .067$$

Exercise #27
Using the Spearman-Brown Formula

$$r_{sb} = \frac{nr_{xy}}{1 + (n-1)r_{xy}}$$

Part 1: Effect on Reliability of Reducing the Length of a Test

A reduction from 150 to 100 items would reduce the reliability coefficient from .89 to .84. Thus, if a test developer or user wanted to reduce by 50 the number of items of this test—one that had a preexisting reliability of .89—it's a good guess that such a reduction can be made without an appreciable loss in reliability of the test.

The solution to Part 1 is as follows:

$$n = \frac{100}{150} = .67$$

$$r_{sb} = \frac{.67(.89)}{1 + (-.33)(.89)} = \frac{.5963}{1 - .2937} = \frac{.5963}{.7063} = .844$$

Part 2: How many items must be added in order to bring a test up to a desired level of reliability?

$$r' = \text{Desired Level of Reliability}$$

$$r_{xx} = \text{Reliability of the Existing Test}$$

$$n = \frac{r'(1 - r_{xx})}{r_{xx}(1 - r')}$$

$$\frac{.80(1 - .60)}{.60(1 - .80)} = \frac{(.80)(.40)}{(.60)(.20)} = \frac{3200}{1200} = 2.67$$

The number of items in the test (with an existing reliability of .60) would have to be increased by a factor of 2.7 (2.67 rounded up to 2.7). If the original test contained 100 items with an $r = .60$, the new test would have to contain a total of 270 items (or 2.7 multiplied by a factor of 100) in order to have a reliability of .80.

Exercise #32
The Multitrait-Multimethod Matrix

A. The reliability of the anxiety measures is very good, at .95 for the Self-Evaluation measure, and .86 for the Coach's Evaluation measure. The reliability of the skill measures is somewhat lower, at .80 for the Self-Evaluation measure, and .71 for the Coach's Evaluation measure. Convergent validity is represented in the correlations between different measures designed to measure the same construct. Convergent validity is good for the two anxiety measures, at .77, but weak for the two skill measures, at .15. These coefficients should be higher than the remaining correlations in the matrix, which represent discriminant validity. This is true for the anxiety measures, which correlate more highly with each other than with the skill measures; correlations between the anxiety and skill measures range from .10 (self-anxiety with coach-skill) to .40 (self-anxiety with self-skill). Thus the anxiety measures seem to possess good construct validity. However, problems in the construct validity of the skill measures become apparent when their convergent validity coefficient is compared with these same discriminant validity coefficients. For example, we see that the self-evaluation of skill correlates higher with the self-evaluation of anxiety (.40) than it does with the coach's evaluation of skill (.15).

In brief, the reliability and construct validity of the anxiety measures seems to be good. The reliability of the skill measures is not as strong, and the construct validity of the skill measures is weak.

B. The reliability coefficients, located on the main diagonal, indicate that (1) both SAT measures are highly reliable, (2) the high school grades are somewhat reliable, and (3) the college grades possess weak reliability.

The three correlations between the various math scores (.77, .73, .78) are relatively high, indicating good convergent validity for the math tests. The three correlations between the various verbal scores (.69, .30, .75) present a more mixed picture. The lowest correlation is between SAT and college scores, indicating that these scores are not closely related.

An evaluation of the discriminant validity coefficients also yields a mixed picture. The situation present with SAT and high school scores is ideal. While correlations are relatively high when SAT math is compared with high school math (.77) and SAT verbal is compared with high school verbal (.69), the correlations are lower between SAT math and high school verbal (.18) and SAT verbal and high school math (.20). These latter values are discriminant validity coefficients. This pattern of convergent validity coefficients that are higher than the discriminant validity coefficients indicates that the two components of the SAT are measuring something specifically related to corresponding components in high school.

The situation with the SAT and college scores is not as clear-cut. Again the convergent validity coefficients (.73 for math, .30 for verbal) are higher than the discriminant validity coefficients (.17 and .10). However, because the convergent validity coefficient for the verbal scores is low, the pattern observed is not as dramatic.

The relationship between the high school and college scores is highly problematic. The convergent validity coefficients (.78 and .75) are both lower than one of the discriminant validity coefficients (.80) and not a lot higher than the other (.66). Thus the high school measures of math and verbal skill are not distinctively related to the college measures of math and verbal skill. This is a construct validity problem.

The only coefficients yet to be discussed are the correlations between verbal and math scores from the same measurement method. SAT verbal and math scores correlate .56, and high school verbal and math scores correlate .55. These coefficients indicate that the two verbal and math scores are not completely distinctive. The fact that these correlations are lower than the convergent validity coefficients is a positive feature. The correlation between college math and verbal scores, at .80, is an anomaly in the matrix provided to challenge the best students. As discussed in Chapter 6 of the text, the correlation between the verbal and math scores, a validity coefficient, is limited by the reliability of the verbal score and the math score. In this case, we see that the validity coefficient is much larger than the reliability coefficients, which is theoretically highly unlikely. It also indicates some important problems for construct validity of the college measures, because verbal and math scores in college correlate better with each other than they do with themselves.

Exercise #33
Factor Analysis and the Correlation Matrix

Students should provide items for W, X, and Y to which highly similar answers would be expected. Item Z should be quite different and should yield answers that are likely to be unrelated to W, X, and Y. For example:

W: What is your current salary?

X: What was your salary last year?

Y: What is your taxable salary, according to the federal government?

Z: How many hours per month do you spend in your car?

Exercise #34
Factor Analysis and Construct Validity

1. Because White and colleagues wanted to understand what the various impulsivity tests are measuring, they chose to include several different impulsivity tests. They selected tests that had published reliability and validity information and seemed interesting from the testtaker's perspective. They purposefully looked for measures that included the viewpoints of various people—while most measures were completed by the subjects of the study, in this case 12- and 13-year-old boys, other tests were designed to be completed about the boys by their teachers, parents, or outside observers. In all, they identified 11 measures of impulsivity.

2. White et al. then selected a sample of 430 boys age 12 and 13 to complete the test. Because the authors are particularly interested in the relationshps between the impulsivity measures and delinquency, approximately half of the boys selelected for the study were known to be at high risk for delinquency.

3. If all of the measures mean the same thing by "impulsivity," and if all are valid, then large and positive correlations would be expected between the different measures.

4. The correlations were all between −.08 and +.33, in what the authors call "the low-to-moderate range" (p. 197). White et al. suggest that these small correlations might indicate the measurement of more than one kind of impulsivity across the different scales.

5. An examination of the factor loadings from the article by White et al. shows that four variables clearly load on the first factor and not on the second factor: impulsivity as rated by the boy, by the parent, and by the teacher, and restlessness as rated by the outside observer. For example, the outside observer's rating of restlessness has a factor loading of .44 on the first factor, but only −.06 on the second factor. This indicates that ratings of restlessness reflect whatever constitutes the first factor but are unrelated to the second factor. A similar pattern is evident for each of the three other impulsivity ratings on this factor.

6. Continuing on with the second factor identified by White and colleagues, six variables clearly load on that factor and not on the first factor: the Trail Making Test, the number of Stroop errors, time perception, the number of cards played in a gambling game, ability to delay gratification, and the slowness with which they could trace a circle. All of these were tasks the boys were asked to complete that required the ability and willingness to direct and control one's thought processes.

7. A variety of answers are acceptable here, but should involve the development of a task of cognitive impulsivity that involves the evaluation of others and/or the development of a task of behavioral impulsivity involving observation rather than self-report or other-report. After development, these tasks should be administered to a new group of boys, along with some of the tasks used by White et al. to determine whether, for example, the observational measure of behavioral impulsivity actually correlates with the other measures of behavioral impulsivity used in the White et al. study.

8. First, the authors have clarified the construct of impulsivity. Just two common factors or dimensions seem to underlie the 11 impulsivity measures included in the analysis; there seems to be a behavioral dimension and a cognitive dimension (or, perhaps, a task dimension and a rating scale dimension). Second, construct validity is demonstrated, particularly for the behavioral dimension of impulsivity, which is related to delinquency in the way that is predicted by relevant theories.

Exercise #39
Item Analysis: Quantitative Methods

2. (b) The probability of guessing correctly on any single item on the basis of chance alone on a multiple-choice item that contains four alternatives is 1/4, or .25, or 25%.

(c) The optimal level of item difficulty for any AHT item can be calculated as follows:

$$\frac{.25 + 1}{2} = \frac{1.25}{2} = .625$$

(d) If 60 of the 100 examinees were correct in their response to Item 47, the item-difficulty index for Item 47 can be calculated as follows:

$$p_{47} = \frac{60}{100} = .60$$

(e) If 69 of the 100 examinees were correct in their response to Item 93, the item-difficulty index for Item 93 can be calculated as follows:

$$p_{93} = \frac{69}{100} = .69$$

(f) Item 47 was more difficult than Item 93; Item 47 had a lower item-difficulty index than Item 93.

(g) The item-score standard deviations for Items 93 and 47 can be calculated as follows:

$$s_{93} = p_{93}(1 - p_{93}) = .69(1 - .69) = .46$$

$$s_{47} = p_{47}(1 - p_{47}) = .60(1 - .60) = .49$$

(h) The item-reliability index for Item 16 can be calculated as follows:

$$(.40)(.75) = .30$$

(i) The item-discrimination index for Items 1 and 2 can be calculated as follows:

$$d_1 = \frac{25 - 8}{27} = \frac{17}{27} = .63$$

$$d_2 = \frac{9 - 14}{27} = \frac{-5}{27} = .185$$

Item 1 is clearly a better item than Item 2; the item-discrimination index for Item 1 is in the high-middle range while the item-discrimination index for Item 2 is negative (and therefore indicative of a problem).

(j) Without resorting to quantitative analysis and simply "eyeballing" the data, it can be seen that Item 2 is not a good item. More members of the low-scoring (L) than the high-scoring (H) group got the item correct. Distractor choice *a* seemed to draw a great number of the testtakers in the *H* group, and one way to begin revising the item might be to discuss it with the members of the *H* group who believed *a* to be the correct answer.

(k) Item 1 is a good item to the extent that the ratio of members of group *H* to group *L* who got the item right was approximately 3 to 1. However, the item could still be improved; distractor choices *b* and *d* fool no one. Also, for the purpose of improving future student learning, the test user might wish to discuss with members of the *L* group what their thinking was with respect to distractor choice *a* since so many of the group members selected this incorrect alternative.

Exercise #43
Interpreting IQ Scores

For the answers to this 10-item true/false test we again turn to Professor John R. Hills.[2]

Answer to Test on IQ Scores

Questions 1–5, 7, and 9 are false. Question 8 and 10 are true. The answer to Question 6 is true or false depending on whose opinion you believe, or how you evaluate empirical data, conjecture, opinion, and hope. Explanations:

1. IQ tests do not measure innate abilities unmodified by environment. It is even questioned whether tests given at birth could be argued to be measures of innate abilities because the fetus is influenced by its environment in many ways.

2. Nearly all IQ scores from current intelligence tests use a deviation IQ based on standard scores with a mean of 100 and a standard deviation of 15 or 16 instead of the ratio IQ score based on MA/CA.

3. Different IQ tests can result in quite different scores for the same person because different IQ tests contain different kinds of items or different relative emphases. Different IQ tests are based on different norms groups, which can also result in different IQs for the same person.

4. IQ scores may change, and sometimes markedly. Cronbach uses as an illustration a person whose IQ changed by 55 points with changes in environment (*Essentials of Psychological Testing*, Third Edition, Harper and Row, p. 232). Other evidence also points to the strong possibility of significant changes in IQ score with changes in the environment or, in the case of older forms of IQ tests, changes in age of the examinee (Ahmann & Glock, *Evaluating Pupil Growth*, Fourth Edition, Allyn and Bacon, pp. 380–390).

5. Although it is true that blacks on the average score 10 to 15 points lower than whites on IQ tests if the content of the items stresses verbal reasoning, there is no clear evidence that the difference is due to bias in the test or its items. Manny's score of 115 is about a standard deviation above average, or at about the 84th percentile. If he had scored 15 points higher, he would have placed about two standard deviations above average, or at about the 98th percentile. Most likely Manny's performance will correspond to his score of 115, not a higher score. It would be a mistake to predict greater success for Manny than would be associated with his score of 115 or to expect his performance in activities depending on verbal reasoning to be comparable to those of students at the 98th percentile instead of comparable to those of students at the 84th percentile. The same kind of interpretation would apply if Manny had scored a standard deviation below the mean, or at IQ 85. We would then recognize that he has more difficulty with verbal reasoning items than average, and most likely he would then have more than average difficulty with the verbal materials he encountered in school unless something occurred to remedy this weakness.

6. Research support for using IQ scores or part scores on intelligence tests for diagnosis of emotional disorders or brain injury is sketchy at best. For example, read Cronbach, op. cit., pages 248–251, or

---

[2]Reprinted with permission from *Hills' Handy Hints* by John R. Hills published by the National Council on Measurement in Education (1986).

Tittle's review of WISC-R in the *Eighth Mental Measurements Yearbook,* page 353. However, the manual for WISC-R indicates that it is useful for psychological diagnosis. So, you could reasonably argue that based on what you have read you deserve credit for either T or F.

7. The variety in colleges and their requirements is surprising to those who have not developed a familiarity with the literature on college admissions. Cronbach (op. cit., p. 219) is a handy reference indicating, for example, that among college entrants studied by Wolfle in the 1950s, 18 percent had IQ scores between 100 and 109. Very few colleges are highly selective; most of them reject only students who are below average, that is, below IQ 100, and most colleges admit some of the applicants who are below average.

8. One cannot count on finding predictive validity data in the test manual for IQ tests. A specific example is the WISC-R. Tittle (*Eighth Mental Measurements Yearbook,* p. 353) states that the major weakness of the WISC-R manual is the discussion of validity. Sax (*Principles of Educational and Psychological Measurement and Evaluation,* Second Edition, Wadsworth, pp. 389–391) points out that neither the WISC manual or the WISC-R manual even mentions the word "validity," and he goes on to indicate that the manuals for group intelligence tests similarly fail to provide information about validity (p. 392).

9. One of the mystiques about IQ scores is that the individual should not know what his IQ score is. Any other score is all right, but not the IQ score. Prior to the 1960s, the same mystique applied to College Board *SAT* scores. I doubt that any educational measurement book espouses such secrecy about any test score. Mehrens and Lehmann (*Measurement and Evaluation in Education and Psychology,* pp. 608–609) firmly state that all achievement and aptitude scores should be disseminated to all professional staff members and to the individuals who were tested, even though they note that according to a study by Goslin, half of teachers surveyed had never given a pupil even a general idea of his intelligence. Remember, IQ scores from modern tests are no more than standard scores on a measure of generalized achievement of cognitive skills and knowledge. They have no special, secret, or magical properties except in the minds of the uninformed.

10. Coaching students for tests of college admission has become an important topic in recent years. Debate continues concerning the effectiveness of coaching for those tests. However, it is often erroneously assumed that IQ tests measure something innate or so fundamental that coaching is ineffective for items on these tests. Some IQ tests include unusual kinds of items for which coaching is beneficial. In fact, some investigators have suggested and demonstrated that IQ scores might be more valid if all children were coached on such items (Cronbach, op. cit., page 245).

Exercise #68
Personality Test Scales

1. Items to be scored on the CR Scale of the MPPI are as follows:
   - 17. True
   - 24. False
   - 32. True
   - 40. True
   - 45. True
   - 47. True
   - 57. True
   - 63. True
   - 78. False

2. In addition to Items #16 and #61, item pairs to be scored on the IN Scale of the MPPI are as follows:

Item #4 and Item #93
Item #5 and Item #94
Item #16 and Item #61
Item #44 and Item #69
Item #53 and Item #76

3. Items to be scored on the Masculinity/Femininity Scale (M/F) of the MMPI are as follows:

27. True (Female) False (Male)
34. True (Female) False (Male)
48. False (Female) True (Male)
84. True (Female) False (Male)
91. False (Female) True (Male)

5. Items to be scored on the Unusual Response Scale (UN-Scale) of the MPPI are as follows:

10. True
17. True
24. False
25. True
31. False
33. True
40. True
45. True
47. True
57. True
63. True
75. True
78. False

6. Items to be scored on the Faking Good Scale (FA+) of the MPPI are as follows:

1. True
7. True
9. False
22. True
68. True

5. Items to be scored on the Faking Bad Scale (FA–) of the MPPI are as follows:

8. True
9. True
11. False
31. False
55. True

Exercise #69
"Just Your Type"

Part 4 Answer Key:

MPPI items that measure endomorphy

15. True
29. False

MPPI items that measure ectomorphy

18. False
36. False

MPPI items that measure mesomorphy

20. True
71. False

Exercise #84
The Multitrait-Multimethod Matrix Revisited

1. Of interest will be those correlations between pairs of scales that are expected to measure the same thing: the correlation between the anxiety scale from the MCMI-II and the anxiety scale from the MMPI, between the depression scale from the MCMI-II and the depression scale from the MMPI, and so on. There are four of these convergent validity coefficients in all, on a downward diagonal in the lower left quadrant of Table 2.

2. The anxiety scales possess high convergent validity, as they correlate .84. The depression and substance abuse scales have a more moderate level of convergent validity, correlating .58 and .40, respectively. Finally, the convergent validity for the two measures of psychotic thought is low, correlating only .19.

3. & 4.   All of the remaining coefficients are relevant to discriminant validity. For illustration, consider the MCMI-II anxiety score. In Table 2, this involves the first column of correlations, with the exception of the correlation already examined for convergent validity. Good discriminant validity seems present relative to two of the MMPI scales (substance dependence correlates –.05 and psychotic thought correlates .00). However, the MCMI-II anxiety scale correlates highly with the MCMI-II depression scale (.94), indicating poor discriminant validity in this area. The correlations of the MCMI-II anxiety scale are also higher-than-desired with the MCMI-II substance dependence measure (.53), the MCMI-II psychosis measure (.75), and the MMPI depression measure (.51). Thus, while the MCMI-II anxiety scale has good convergent validity with the MMPI measure, the scale lacks discriminant validity, indicating (more generally) a problem with construct validity.

Now consider the discriminant validity of the remaining three MCMI-II scales included in Table 2. For each clinical syndrome, there are six discriminant validity coefficients—two for each of the three clinical syndromes different from the one represented on the MCMI-II scale that you are considering. All three remaining MCMI-II scales demonstrate weak discriminant validity, because each correlates more highly with other MCMI-II scales than with the corresponding MMPI scale. For example, the MCMI-II substance dependence scale correlates .53 with the MCMI-II anxiety scale, .56 with the MCMI-II depression scale, and .62 with the MCMI-II psychotic thought scale, all greater than the correlation of .40 with the MMPI measure of substance dependence. The three remaining coefficients relevant to the discriminant validity of the MCMI-II substance dependence scales are the correlations with the MMPI measures of anxiety (.51), depression (.08), and psychosis (.47). Again, two of these three correlations are greater than the convergent validity coefficient for the substance abuse scale. As McCann (1990) notes, these data cast doubt on the construct validity of these MCMI-II scales.

This example illustrates the importance of examining both the discriminant and convergent validity of psychological tests. Often researchers report information about convergent validity, with little or no data about discriminant validity. Although some of the MCMI-II measures have good convergent validity, examination of their discriminant validity leads to questions about the scales' construct validity. The importance of this difficulty becomes clear when we ask about what construct is reflected in a high MCMI-II anxiety score. That score will generally accompany a high MCMI-II depression score, because the two scales are so highly correlated. This makes interpretation difficult: a person with a high anxiety score could be anxious, depressed, or both. The test does not help with making these distinctions. Such psychometric difficulties, then, have practical implications for the use of these measures in understanding testtakers.